POLICY AND PRACTICE IN HEALTH AND SOCIAL CARE
NUMBER EIGHTEEN

Social Work with Fathers: Positive Practice

POLICY AND PRACTICE IN HEALTH AND SOCIAL CARE

1: Jacqueline Atkinson, *Private and Public Protection: Civil Mental Health Legislation* (2006)

2: Charlotte Pearson (ed.), *Direct Payments and Personalisation of Care* (2006)

3: Joyce Cavaye, *Hidden Carers* (2006)

4: Mo McPhail (ed.), *Service User and Carer Involvement: Beyond Good Intentions* (2007)

5: Anne Stafford, *Safeguarding and Protecting Children and Young People* (2008)

6: Alison Petch, *Health and Social Care: Establishing a Joint Future?* (2007)

7: Gillian MacIntyre, *Learning Disability and Social Inclusion* (2008)

8: Ailsa Cook, *Dementia and Well-being: Possibilities and Challenges* (2008)

9: Michele Burman and Jenny Johnstone (eds), *Youth Justice* (2009)

10: Rebecca L. Jones and Richard Ward (eds), *LGBT Issues: Looking Beyond Categories* (2009)

11: Jacqueline H. Watts, *Death, Dying and Bereavement: Issues for Practice* (2009)

12: Richard Hammersley and Phil Dalgarno, *Drugs* (2012)

13: Ailsa Stewart, *Supporting Vulnerable Adults: Citizenship, Capacity, Choice* (2012)

14: Emma Miller, *Individual Outcomes: Getting Back to What Matters* (2012)

15: Ken Barrie, *Alcohol* (2012)

16: Gary Clapton and Pauline Hoggan, *Adoption and Fostering in Scotland* (2012)

17: Graham Connelly and Ian Milligan, *Residential Child Care: Between Home and Family* (2012)

18: Gary Clapton, *Social Work with Fathers: Positive Practice* (2013)

POLICY AND PRACTICE IN HEALTH AND SOCIAL CARE

SERIES EDITORS

JOYCE CAVAYE and ALISON PETCH

Social Work with Fathers: Positive Practice

Gary Clapton

Senior Lecturer

School of Social and Political Science

University of Edinburgh

EDINBURGH ◆ LONDON

First published in 2013 by
Dunedin Academic Press Ltd

Head Office:
Hudson House, 8 Albany Street,
Edinburgh EH1 3QB

London Office:
The Towers, 54 Vartry Road,
London N15 6PU

ISBN 978-1-780460-08-6

British Library Cataloguing in Publication Data
A catalogue record for this book is available from the British Library

Typeset by Makar Publishing Production
Printed by CPI Group (UK) Ltd., Croydon, CR0 4YY

CONTENTS

Series Editors' Introduction vi

Acknowledgements viii

List of Abbreviations ix

Introduction x

Chapter 1 Defining Fathers, Fathering and Fatherhood(s) 1

Chapter 2 At Odds with the Evidence: The Benefits of Positive Father Involvement … and Social Work Practice and Policymakers 9

Chapter 3 Reaching and Engaging Fathers 25

Chapter 4 Working with Fathers 36

Chapter 5 Assessing and Working with Risk with Fathers 55

Chapter 6 Positive Agency and Teaching Practice with Fathers 72

Chapter 7 For Fathers' Workers 83

Some Last Words 94

References 96

Index 108

SERIES EDITORS' INTRODUCTION

Fathers can be a shadowy presence in day-to-day social work practice. Work with children and families can often, by default, become work primarily with children and mothers. Moreover, in recent years, the move to fully acknowledge and credit the contribution of women to society as a whole has tended to favour a spotlight on mothers. This volume provides an important redress, arguing that health and social policy in general and social work in particular need to become much more sensitive to the critical role of the father. This should recognise that a father can be a resource, a risk or, indeed, both a resource and a risk. Through carefully presented vignettes Gary Clapton illustrates the opportunities to work more positively with fathers and to ensure that child and family policies do not, by default, become inappropriately skewed.

An introductory chapter captures some of the changing demographic and image of fatherhood over recent years and highlights the wide range of categories and involvement embraced by the term. Chapter 2 explores both the benefits of engagement with fathers and the barriers, particularly for social work practice, of doing so. Strategies for overcoming this exclusion, and at times hostility, are outlined in Chapter 3, where the focus is on reaching and engaging fathers. Chapter 4 examines in more detail the approaches to working with fathers, emphasising the benefits of a strengths-based approach, one building on the positive contribution that men can make to their children's lives. Specific attention is given to young fathers, to non-resident fathers, to fathers in prison and to lone fathers. The important issue of risk and of the need for appropriate assessment is addressed in Chapter 5, emphasising again, however, the importance of an approach based on positive practice.

Having presented an evidence-based argument for the approach, the final chapters explore how the model of positive practice with fathers can be embedded at team and agency level. The author has an obvious passion for his subject; however, the achievement of this volume is that it presents a reasoned argument not a polemic. Therefore its strength is all the greater.

Dr Joyce Cavaye
Faculty of Health and Social Care, The Open University in Scotland, Edinburgh

Professor Alison Petch
The Institute for Research and Innovation in Social Services (IRISS), Glasgow

ACKNOWLEDGEMENTS

This book would not have been possible without Jane, Lawrie and Jamie in my life, so a huge thanks to them. Thanks also go to Fathers Network Scotland. Finally thanks to Maggie Mellon for her constant love and support.

LIST OF ABBREVIATIONS

ACYF	Administration on Children, Youth and Families
ADHD	Attention deficit hyperactivity disorder
CAF	common assessment framework
CRFR	Centre for Research on Family Relationships
CWDC	Children's Workforce Development Council
DADS	Developing a Daddy Survey
DCSF	Department for Children, Schools and Families
EHRC	Equality and Human Rights Commission
ESCR	Economic and social Research Council
FGC	Family Group Conferences
FNF	Families Need Fathers
FNS	Fathers Network Scotland
FRG	Family Rights Group
HMSO	Her Majesty's Stationery Office
JRF	Joseph Rowntree Foundation
NCT	National Childbirth Trust
TAC	team around the child

INTRODUCTION

Parenting is important to men, and fathers are important to their children and families. The underpinning belief of this book is one that understands the benefits of father-inclusive practice and one of optimism about social work with the vast majority of fathers and their children and families. It is also realistic and practical about those fathers whose behaviour makes it hard to be positive.

While not intending to favour or prioritise one way of being a father or 'doing' fathering among the possibilities that exist, the positive practice in this book concerns the men who accept – or are ascribed – parental responsibility for a child, or would do so if given the opportunity.

The book is about reaching out to, engaging and then working with fathers. It is strengths-based rather than deficit-driven. It also addresses agency practices, trainers and educators. Fathers' workers and support groups are included because of the growing resources that they provide. Firstly, however, the beginning two chapters outline some crucial contexts. These are the striking changes that have taken place in fathers' behaviour, the intersection of fatherhood and masculinity and what we know about the contribution positive fathering can make in the lives of children, women and families. This foreground concludes with the way that fathers have been overlooked by professionals and policymakers and the negative manner in which they are depicted.

Changing fathers

Fathers now play a more active role in childcare and domestic life in general. While fathers still do less of the parenting than mothers, their involvement has grown and continues to grow. Fathers' involvement in childcare has increased from less than fifteen minutes a day in the mid-1970s to three hours a day during the week by the late 1990s, with more at the weekend. Fathers now do a third of parental childcare, which is an eightfold increase in a generation for fathers of preschool children (O'Brien, 2005).

Overall, there have been major shifts in the manner in which fatherhood is thought of and a growing emphasis on what might be described as the 'new father' who actively participates in the care of his child, values girls as of equal worth to boys and engages with the child as an infant rather than remaining on the sidelines until the child is older (Haywood and Mac an Ghail, 2003).

In the twenty-first century, fathers come in all shapes, sizes and colours. While some biological fathers do not 'do' fathering, other non-biological fathers can and do: for example, grandfathers/uncles, foster fathers, adoptive fathers and stepfathers (the last in increasing numbers – Sullivan and Dex, 2009). Today's father is no longer always the traditional (perhaps stereotyped) married breadwinner and disciplinarian in the family. He can be single or married; externally employed or a stay-at home father; gay or straight; an adoptive or step-parent; and a more than capable caregiver to children as they face the various challenges that come with growing up.

Changing expectations

Changes in the law (in 2003) have given parental responsibility to fathers named on their children's birth certificates, whether or not they are married to the mothers. This reflects an emerging emphasis on the preservation of children's relationships with biological and social fathers (Trinder and Lamb, 2005). The extension of paternal leave is also an indicator of growing acknowledgement – and expectation – at governmental level of the importance of fathers in the lives of their children. The issue of fathers has risen on the agenda of politicians and policymakers in recent years. In 1998 the then UK government's Supporting Families initiative made it clear that: 'fathers have a crucial role to play in their children's upbringing.' This momentum has continued with leading government ministers emphasising the importance of fathers:

> I want to see a revolution in how teachers, midwives, doctors, early years and all children's services staff routinely talk to and provide opportunities for the involvement, not only of

> mothers but also fathers, from pregnancy and right through childhood and adolescence (Hughes, 2008).

In a speech to the Fatherhood Institute in 2010, the minister in charge of UK children and families services said:

> It seems to me that there is still a real risk here that dads will continue to be passively discriminated against by public services unless we take action. We already know, for instance, that many men are left feeling somewhat disenfranchised by child health and family services. But I'd suggest that it goes a little deeper than that – to the point where we very often forget fathers altogether when we are dealing with family issues (Loughton, 2010)

At a government level in Scotland, something of this concern and interest has also emerged with the involvement of fathers and fathers' groups in the shaping of a national parenting strategy and is also betokened in the remarks of the Scottish government's minister for children and young people on Fathers Day 2012:

> Dads being fully involved in their children's lives has all sorts of positive benefits for the wider family and community. However, we need to go further to ensure that as a society we truly value and support dads in the role that they play. As we celebrate Father's Day, it's a good time to reflect on what all this means for dads, because sometimes when we talk about parents, we tend to mean mums, and cut dads out of the picture (Campbell, 2012).

At the level of family, expectations have also shifted, with the division between work and childcare no longer conceived along traditional lines by the majority of modern parents. Now only 29% of parents believe that childcare is the primary responsibility of the mother (Ellison *et al.*, 2009).

Changing images: Sensitive dad and brute

Examples of men demonstrating 'softer' emotions have become widespread and feed into the dynamic of changing expectations of fathers. From Paul Gascoigne's tears during the 1990 World Cup to Ken Livingstone's weeping at the launch of his 2012 campaign to become London mayor, we are accepting men's public displays of vulnerability and expressing and talking about themselves in relatively new, at least in public, terms:

> I had been talking to him, and I had built up a wee bit of a rapport, so I just went up to him and I put my arm round him. And he was kind of stamping his feet but he went to his bed without any problem (former Paisley construction worker in training to become a residential childcare worker, quoted in Smith *et al.*, 2011, p. 28).

Yet, alongside the discovery of the New Man Dad, there have been other more negative discourses, such as that of the father who won't lift a finger (or lifts his hand too often), the feckless men who father children then abandon them and their mothers, teenage fathers (see, for example, Prime Minister David Cameron's 2011 Fathers Day remark: 'It's high time runaway dads were stigmatised and the full force of shame was heaped upon them') and 'absent'/'non-resident' fathers in general. And there is no end of depictions of brutal Scottish fathers:

> Those Scottish fathers. Not for nothing their wives cried, not for nothing their kids. Cities of night above those five o'clock shadows. Men gone way too sick for the talking. And how they lived in the dark for us now. Or lived in our faces, long denied (O'Hagan, 1999, p. 53).

In John Burnside's 2006 memoir of his life at home, *A Lie About My Father*, his father is mean, a drunk, taciturn, unpredictable, physically ruthless and casually cruel (a favourite teddy is thrown on the fire to teach a lesson about not leaving toys lying around); see also Peter Mullen's brutalising and brutalised father in his film *Neds* (2010). Though these stereotypical fathers undoubtedly existed, they are perhaps notable for being the exception and not the rule.

Now it seems fair to say without fear of contradiction that widespread notions of fathers as distant or bullies, the men who administer punishment ('wait 'til your father gets home') or as incompetent, no longer hold sway. This is not to say that depending on political and social circumstances unfair stereotypes do not emerge, it is just that on a big level we now know more about what good fathering can be and expect more.

Child welfare and protection and fathers

Paradoxically, it seems that the very organisations and institutions that provide services to children and families are those that have been caught unaware by the arrival of fathers in a territory that, until now, has been more or less occupied by welfare agencies focus on mothers. This focus has led to an empty space where good practice in working with fathers should be developed.

Indeed, social work services for families have often been driven by a deficit model of assessment and engagement, i.e. one that starts with an assessment of their failings and proceeds to try to fix these. The ethos of this book, on working with fathers, is different. The selection of research is underpinned by a strengths-based approach, one that emphasises fathers' personal strengths and capacities for positive involvement with their families, partners and children.

I have tried to distil the most relevant research and the most recurring of practical tips and suggestions from within the UK and overseas. It has been a narrow line to walk between a selective literature review or a 'how to' guide. However, the process has been enjoyable, and it is hoped that the reading experience will be too. But more than anything else, this book will be successful if it contributes to the development of positive practice with fathers. Chapter 1 begins with what is meant by the terms 'father' and 'fatherhood' and where these intersect with the question of masculinity and manhood.

CHAPTER 1

Defining Fathers, Fathering and Fatherhood(s)

'There is no one fatherhood' (Dermott, 2008, p. 24).

It has been argued that fatherhood is significantly more fragmented than motherhood (Sheldon, 2007). Without doubt, there are a number of roles (or activities) that can claim the title of father or fathering behaviour. Previously and conventionally, the traditional definition of father was the biological father and adult carer of a child who was married to the child's mother. Closer examination of changing social and familial practices has shown that there are a number of claims to the role of father.

Some key definitions

The Minnesota Fathers and Families Network has produced a useful list of various types of fathers, and with amendments to reflect UK laws and practices this comprises of twelve categories:

- *Legal father* A legal father is the man the law recognises as the father of the child. A legal father may or may not be the child's biological father.
- *Biological father* As legally defined, a biological father is the man with whom a child's mother becomes pregnant. A biological father contributes one-half of a child's genetic heritage. This category includes the fathers of children conceived by donor insemination.
- *Putative father* A term less used (but may be more frequently found in old case notes) that describes a man

who may be a child's biological father but where paternity has not been established.

- *Presumed father* A man is presumed to be the biological father of a child if he and the child's biological mother are or have been married to each other and the child is born during the marriage.
- *Adoptive father* An adoptive father is a man who legally adopts a child of other parents as his own.
- *Stepfather* A stepfather is the husband/partner of the child's mother. The child's biological parents are usually the stepfather's wife/partner and another man, generally from a previous relationship.
- *Foster father* A foster father is, legally, a man who takes a father's place in the nurture and care of a child. A foster father is neither a biological father nor an adoptive father of the child for whom he has caring responsibility.
- *Social father* A social father is a cultural term for a man who takes *de facto* responsibility for a child. This is discussed below.
- *Custodial father and non-custodial father* A custodial father maintains legal custody of a minor child. Legal custody gives parents the right to decide how to raise their child. Parents can share legal custody of their child. A custodial father maintains primary physical care and custody of his minor child. A non-custodial father does not maintain primary care of his minor child. Custody is legally determined and is not necessarily equivalent to the child's residency with him.
- *Resident father and non-resident father* A resident father is one who lives in the same household as his child. A non-resident father is one who lives separately from his child. A non-resident father may be divorced, separated or never-married to the child's mother.
- *Lone father* A single parent is defined through marital status by being never-married, divorced, a widower or with spouse absent. A single parent may or may not live with an unmarried partner or another adult. 'Single', in

the context of 'single parent family/household', means only one parent is present in the home.

- *Father-figure* A term used to describe any man who 'responds to and is a significant influence in forming a child's future' (Giveans and Robinson, 1992, p. 11). Father-figures include friends of the family, relatives and can mean teachers or others that act in such capacity, e.g. sports coaches (adapted from Minnesota Fathers & Families Network, 2007).

Clearly many of these roles are not exclusive and neither does inhabiting one of these roles (e.g. biological father, divorced father) mean that a father does not necessarily care for the child (non-residence may not equate with not caring). Nor are these roles always fixed: for example, the biological father may enter – or re-enter – a child's life and that of its family, producing a situation where there are two fathers.

Involvement

As expected, the definition of paternal involvement has proved to be complex. There are no definitions of paternal involvement that fully capture the varied cultural scripts or lived experiences of fathers, and this has been the subject of much discussion. Lamb *et al.* set an enduring template for categorising father involvement as:

- interaction – the most encouraging type of involvement; involves actual one-on-one interaction between the father and his child. This is measured by observation of the father's direct contact with his child through caretaking and shared activities;
- availability – a more indirect form of involvement; implies the father is physically available or accessible to the child and can easily be reached or approached whether or not direct interaction is occurring;
- responsibility – reflects the extent to which the father oversees total child well-being and care-giving activities. The father's role is to determine how the child is to be taken care of and that necessary resources are available to the child. This form of involvement requires more non-physical interactions (Lamb *et al.*, 1987, pp. 126–9).

However, in their important research review, Lewis and Lamb (2007) suggest that such definitions of fathering, in emphasising care-giving, have tended to neglect breadwinning.

A continuum of paternal involvement has been advanced that deepens and expands notions of paternal involvement from the above three domains of Lamb *et al.* (1987) to fifteen aspects. These include communication, teaching, monitoring, thought processes, errands, caregiving, child-related material support (e.g. financial maintenance, but not only this), shared interests, availability, planning, shared activities, providing, affection, protection and emotional support (Palkovitz, 2002). Lewis and Lamb suggest that 'the list of possible aspects could probably be much longer than this' (Lewis and Lamb, 2007, p. 2). Echoing Palkovitz, who argues that conceptions of paternal involvement ought to be expanded to include the thought processes and emotional experiences of fathers, Lewis and Lamb cite Morgan (1998) who goes further and:

> has provided insights by questioning dimensions of the familiar dichotomy between parenting and activities outside the home. For example, he suggests that participation in trade union activities may serve to protect opportunities in the labour force for the next generation. They could, therefore, be construed as 'fathering', affecting children's long-term well-being (Lewis and Lamb, 2007, p. 2).

Lewis and Lamb (2007) also highlight the work of Lee (2005) who has studied the number and nature of the pathways that men follow in their parental careers. In Lee's analysis:

> Each father's career is charted by the number and nature of their parenting transitions. For example, the trajectory BIO -- NR -- STEP -- DUAL describes a man who resides with his child[ren], then leaves the household, becomes a stepfather and then becomes a biological father again with a new partner (Lewis and Lamb, 2007, p. 16).

They go on to note that: 'In all, Lee has identified seventy-three different pathways in the sample, thereby demonstrating that diversity is indeed the order of the day' (Lewis and Lamb, 2007, p. 16). Lewis and Lamb suggest that there are eight major drivers that influence father involvement. These are:

- biological;
- motivation;
- cultural;
- economic;
- historical;
- legal;
- social policy;
- relationship with mother.

These, Lewis and Lamb (2007) argue, are not fixed but change over time and across cultures with macro shifts, such as rising female participation in the workforce being a cross-cutting factor influencing father involvement. Thus defining fathering proves complex and, probably inevitably, a fixed definition proves elusive.

Terminology also presents a challenge: father, stepfather, 'natural' father, babyfather, birth father, father-figure, father-substitute are all possible and in day-to-day use. In one effort to find a working term for fathers who commit to caring for their children and families, the term 'household father' has been used (Livia Sz *et al.*, 2002). However, this carries with it connotations of alternative lifestyles and the suggestion that fathering is done within four walls and has not become popular.

Therefore, establishing a working definition of father and what constitutes father involvement is fraught with pitfalls but is easier if this is judged in the context of the child and family who relate to him and to which he relates (though this may not be mutually understood to the same degrees!). Where there is no clear biological or legal attribution of father, men are often called social fathers, a term that extends to 'men … who provide a significant degree of nurturance, moral and ethical guidance, companionship, emotional support, and financial responsibility in the lives of children (Connor *et al.*, 2006, p. 6).

In the vast majority of cases, when there is no obvious person doing the fathering, the biological father's whereabouts and potential involvement may be explored by social workers (for the same reasons as the whereabouts/potential involvement of the biological mother may be where there is no mother-figure accepting caring responsibility). The reason for raising the *potential* primacy of the biological father is the assumed possibility of paternal emotional attachment that may be present (Amato and Sobolewski, 2004) or the potential for reconnection with their child with whom a biological father may have had little or no contact (Clapton, 2003a). Generally, these fathers are often ignored or marginalised on many levels of social work (Sonenstein *et al.*, 2002) and they may – when the work is done, when the assessments are successfully undertaken, and the relationship supported and encouraged – be most likely to respond favourably (Ryan, 2000).

This book assumes that the vast majority of fathers, whether biological or otherwise, try to act in good faith, and therefore in the main it is addressed to improving positive practice with those men. However, before we can proceed, the inescapable fact that fathers are also men does need to be addressed.

Fatherhood and masculinity

Fatherhood and masculinity are connected, yet, until recently, the masculinities literature could be considered 'father blind' while the fatherhood literature has engaged very little with the literature on masculinities (Featherstone *et al.*, 2007, p. 86). The briefest of examinations shows that masculinity proves to be as difficult to define as fatherhood. Like the latter, there are as many definitions of masculinity as there are nations, cultures, classes, ethnicities, religions and sexualities. The canon of men and masculinities studies is now extensive (Edwards, 2006), but some things stand out. The prevailing definition of masculinities has been shaped by feminism, and this posits a consistent thread of male power over women. Whether or not a man has power in relation to anything else in his life, he 'enjoys' what has been described as the 'patriarchal dividend' (see for example, Connell, 1995) expressed as benefits, or the potential of these, which are accessible to him and not to a woman in the same position. However, an example of the fluidity of the gender debates is that the notion of the patriarchal dividend has been qualified to be that of a 'patriarchal bargain' in which women participate and the idea of a monolithic patriarchy has thus been questioned (Kandiyoti, 1988). In a similar vein, others have remarked:

> While it is unquestionably the case that many men do occupy positions of power, it is one thing to name those subject positions and another to go on to presume that all men have access to these positions or indeed want to take them up (Cornwall, 2000, p. 23).

Three things seem to have been agreed. Firstly, that masculinity is a social construction. Secondly, that there is no one masculinity, and this has led to writers in the field adopting the term 'masculinities' (Kimmel *et al.*, 2005) and that gender equality has yet to arrive. Consensus ceases there: debate is continuous. However, work on the connections between fatherhood and masculinities remains thin (Marsiglio and Pleck, 2005).

What can be said without too much disagreement is that, while all fathers contain within their identities aspects of masculinity, not all men are fathers. So it is possible to be a man but not a father but impossible to be a father and not a man. Because the *assumption* of fatherhood is a social act distinct from the acknowledgement of fatherhood (e.g. via the biological act of participation in creation), then deciding to *be* a father and 'do' fathering can be characterised as a positive expression of masculinity. In the words of one writer, fatherhood is 'one of those situations where masculinity is, as it were, on the line' (Morgan, 1992, p. 99). Here, it is acknowledged that, on occasions, the assumption or exercise of fatherhood may not be a benign act: for example, in contested contact where 'father's rights' may be asserted as a means of settling scores with the mother of the child, with the welfare of the child being only a secondary consideration. However, this book is concerned first and foremost to maximise the positively involved father dimension of masculinity as in the interests of everyone – men, women and children. Men's assumption of, and transition to, parenting and active involvement with their children can help many men develop more nurturing personality traits (Hawkins and Belsky, 1989) and boost self-esteem (Barker, 2006). Palkovitz sums up some of the gains for men:

> It is fathers' ongoing exposure to alternative perspectives, contingencies, emotions, demands, interactions, wishes, desires, fears, hurts, dreams, friendships, and needs that pull men toward new levels of developmental functioning. When a man commits his life to fathering, in many regards, the child becomes father to the man (Palkovitz, 2002, p. 5).

Young fathers, whose experiences and position have come to the fore recently, have been specifically identified as having much to gain, primarily meaning and purpose in their lives, and a stronger sense of identity and self-worth by embracing fatherhood (Kiselica, 2008). Additionally, greater nurturing by men is a contribution to greater male and female labour equity in domestic life and childcare (Ruxton, 2004). Thus, not only children stand to benefit from positively involved fathering, so too do men and women.

****

Having outlined the various ways that men can be fathers and established the importance that being a father is to men, the next chapter asks 'what is the good that fathers bring to the lives of children, women and families?'. It also discusses the less than helpful ways in which fathers have been regarded by professionals and draws attention to the negativity and lack of inclusion in policy.

Key research and resources

Understanding fatherhood: A review of recent research, Joseph Rowntree Foundation (2007). Available at URL: www.jrf.org.uk/sites/files/jrf/understanding-fatherhood.pdf (accessed 17 December 2012)

The Developing a Daddy Survey (DADS) Project: Framework Paper (2004) especially pp. 13–21 on 'Conceptualizing father involvement'. Available at URL: www.childtrends.org/Files/Child_Trends-2004_12_01_ES_NICHDDads.pdf (accessed 17 December 2012)

CHAPTER 2

At Odds with the Evidence: The Benefits of Positive Father Involvement ... and Social Work Practice and Policymakers

> 'Current service provision in the UK for vulnerable families is generally based on an assumption at *odds with the evidence* and with the child's perspective – that fatherhood is an optional and marginally significant "add-on" for children, unlike motherhood, which is an essential' (Fathers Direct, 2008, p. 79).

Writing a book about the value of involving mothers in their children's lives and welfare would seem ridiculous, yet there is much evidence to suggest that social work and social workers remain unconvinced as to the involvement of a child's other parent – the father. This chapter seeks to convince.

Research on fathers and fatherhood gained momentum in the UK throughout the 1990s and has built up a substantial body of knowledge on which some broad and convincing statements can be made. Research often tells us what we instinctively know, and this is the case with fathers. Encouraging the active engagement of fathers in families is good social work practice. The positive involvement of fathers is of benefit to children, women and fathers themselves. Research has also conclusively rejected any notion that fathers are inessential in the lives of families and children. What follows is a review of this evidence as to why social workers ought to take fathers seriously, as well as a discussion of the barriers to this.

The benefits and impact

Education, schooling and teenage years

Dennis and Erdos found unemployed fathers' support for their children's education strongly connected with those children's escape from disadvantage (Dennis and Erdos, 1992). Since then, major studies across the world which follow families over time have found fathers' involvement with their children linked with their higher educational achievement and higher educational/occupational mobility relative to their parents (Pleck and Masciadrelli, 2004; Flouri, 2005; Sarkadi *et al.*, 2008). For example, in the UK, fathers' involvement with their seven- and eleven-year-old children is linked with their better educational attainment at age twenty (Flouri and Buchanan, 2002). This is as true for daughters as for sons, across all social classes – and whether the mother is highly involved too, or not. More recently, a father's interest in his child's education, particularly at age eleven, has been found to have more influence on education success than family background, the child's personality or poverty (Hango, 2007). Blanden (2006) found the opposite also the case, i.e. that low fatherly interest was similarly predictive – a father's low interest in his son's education reduces his boy's chances of escaping poverty by 25% (research such as this tells us the detrimental outcomes of poor or negative father involvement and is equally powerful in the case for why social workers should not ignore fathers).

Fathers' (higher) commitment to their child's education and their involvement with the school are also associated with children's better behaviour at school, including reduced risk of suspension or expulsion (Goldman, 2005). Children's school behaviour is strongly linked with their educational attainment; and fathers' influence on that behaviour is not only significant (Lloyd *et al.*, 2003; Velleman, 2004) but may also at times be more significant than mothers': for example, fathers' harsh parenting is more strongly linked to children's (especially boys') aggression than is mothers' harsh parenting (Chang *et al.*, 2003).

It has been indicated that a teenager's sense of self-worth is predicted by the quality of their early childhood play with their father, and there are links between a father's involvement at the age of seven and lower levels of later police contact as reported by mothers and teachers (Lewis and Lamb, 2007).

Father involvement and the effects on children's later lives

In the UK, high levels of father involvement at ages seven and eleven were found to protect against experience of homelessness in the adult sons of manual workers (Flouri, 2005). Flouri and Buchanan earlier discovered that father and adolescent reports of their closeness at age sixteen correlated with measures of the child's depression and marital satisfaction at age thirty-three (Flouri and Buchanan, 2002). Harris *et al.* (1998) found that both low father involvement and decreasing closeness in adolescence predicted delinquency in adult life, and Blanden (2006) discovered that low father involvement (e.g. in his son's education) reduces the child's chances of escaping poverty.

Other research has shown that the benefits of father involvement can remain in cases where the father is not resident with the child. In separated families, high levels of non-resident father involvement protect against later mental health problems in children (Flouri, 2005). On the other hand, controlling for other factors, absent fatherhood has been shown negatively to affect children directly: for example, by contributing to their difficulties with peer relationships, including bullying (Parke *et al.*, 2004); and, indirectly, via increased maternal stress and reduced income (McLanahan and Teitler, 1999).

Research involving particular categories of fathers seems to be equally clear about the importance of their involvement: for example, Zelenko *et al.* (2001) found that ignoring young fathers may compromise children's well-being, because, among expectant teenage mothers, lack of perceived support by fathers correlated with high scores on a Child Abuse Potential Inventory. Kalil *et al.* (2005) report that a decreased involvement by young fathers is significantly associated with young mothers' increased parenting stress. Regarding fathers not resident with their children, research indicates that:

> the amount of time fathers spend with their children is not as important as the quality of this time, however. A child who has a close and supportive relationship with his or her father

> is more likely to do well in adulthood regardless of whether or not he or she lives with him when they are growing up (Asmussen and Weizel, 2010, p. 5).

As the Fatherhood Institute notes, the benefits of father involvement are not just true for middle-class families but rather that 'whatever the father's education level, his interest and participation pay off for his children' (Fatherhood Institute, 2010a, p. 2).

The benefits of involved fathering extend beyond those that accrue to the child. Mothers and fathers themselves have been found to gain when fathers are included.

Father involvement and mothers

Neglect or abuse is still overwhelmingly regarded as a failure of mothering. Therefore, a failure to include fathers means that one parent – the mother – bears the unfair burden of investigation, and of responsibility. In relation to youth offending, for example, Page *et al.* found that: 'the courts were seen as not adequately ensuring that fathers were present whenever possible with the result that parenting orders and parenting contracts tended to be applied to mothers much more frequently than fathers' (Page *et al.*, 2008, p. 7).

The same consequences of omission apply to other services, such the Scottish Children's Hearings system, in which a similar lack of involvement of fathers has placed an unfair burden on mothers (Gillies, 2004). In respect of this particular service, until recently unmarried fathers who were not resident with their child were not automatically included in those invited to a Hearing (Plumtree, 2011).

Pleck (2007) points out that father involvement can influence child development in a number of ways: for example, in addition to direct effects, indirect effects on children may be brought about through father involvement influencing mothering practice. In their study of fathers and child protection, Ferguson and Hogan found that:

> Involved fatherhood benefits mothers as well as children. In general, the mothers we interviewed wanted the men to be actively involved fathers and felt that intervention work had developed the men's capacities to nurture and

> take domestic responsibility. Mothers felt that intervention brought considerable benefits to themselves, by helping to produce men who shared parenting, and were physically and emotionally available to them (Ferguson and Hogan, 2004, p. 153).

It is no coincidence then that higher father involvement is linked with lower parenting stress and depression in mothers (Fisher *et al.*, 2006) and, ultimately, failure to engage with fathers makes mothers unfairly responsible for change in families, and can compromise their welfare and safety.

Father involvement and fathers

The Fatherhood Institute has summarised some of the benefits to fathers of greater involvement. These include:

> Positive changes from parent education have been recorded in fathers' (including young and imprisoned fathers') communication skills, sensitivity to babies' cues, parenting attitudes, knowledge of child development, acceptance of the child, confidence, satisfaction and self-efficacy as parents; self-perception and self-esteem; parenting stress; positive emotionality towards their children; and commitment to parenting. Some fathers have used parenting support as a route into education, training and employment (Fatherhood Institute, 2009b, p. 4).

There are many other benefits that speak even more directly to men's self-improvement: for example, more involved fatherhood has been shown to turn men away from crime and self-harm and to be effective in preventing recidivism among men in prison. These and other such benefits for men will be returned to throughout the chapters in this book.

Child protection

Child welfare and protection and fathers is a major theme that runs throughout this book, and every chapter will pay some attention to this, in particular Chapter 5, which is given over to discussing risk, child protection and fathers. This brief section confines itself to what research tells us about the value of child protection practitioners engaging with fathers. In child protection, as in other settings, most children want contact with most fathers (Scourfield, 2006); and the strength and complexity of these children's attachments to significant adults, including fathers and father-figures, should not be underestimated (Daniel and Taylor, 2001).

In the UK, £3 billion a year is currently spent on children by local authority social services, of which more than £1 billion goes to residential provision (Hirsch, 2006). It is likely that these costs could be substantially reduced were fathers and paternal relatives systematically involved in care proceedings. In an important contribution relating to care proceedings Bellamy concludes that: 'The identified relationship between the involvement of a non-custodial parent, most often a biological father, and a reduction in the likelihood that children are placed into out-of-home care, is a unique finding' (Bellamy, 2009, p. 260).

Vulnerable children seem to be in the greatest need of ongoing positive relationships with their fathers. They tend to do worse than better supported children when father–child relationships are poor or non-existent; and they seem to experience greater benefits when a relationship with a biological father and/or father-figure is positive (Dunn *et al.*, 2004).

To sum up then, from the point of view of children and families practitioners, the benefits of engagement with fathers are:

- the potential for children's welfare and mother's support is maximised:
- there are more 'eyes' to survey the well-being of the child:
- paternal networks are engaged as possible, alternative permanency options:
- as well as enhanced resources, there is an improved risk assessment, because it is more comprehensive than when focusing solely on the mother.

If these are the benefits, what are the obstacles to the research findings becoming practice?

Social work practice and policy attitudes

Practice attitudes

The overwhelming barrier to developing positive practice with fathers is the gulf between what research tells us and thinking, attitudes and practice on the ground. And, as we shall see, what is on the ground presents a challenge, because while there is some evidence of positive policy developments it remains the case that:

> most local authorities did not appear to have taken a 'strategic lead' on supporting fathers in family services in their area. Rather, any local practice had generally developed sporadically and was the result of specific managers and practitioners taking an interest in the issue. Father-inclusive practice was not seen to be routine or mainstream in family services (Page *et al.*, 2008, p. 6).

Lack of inclusion

Across a range of children and family services there is evidence of such a lack of inclusion. In her study of *adoption* services, Neil found notable that:

> about the birthfathers of children in all three groups is the paucity of information that social workers were able to supply. In 17% of cases the identity of the father was unknown to the social worker, either because the mother did not know who the father was or because she chose not to tell the agency. In further situations it appeared that agencies had known the identity of the father but had not tried to engage him in the adoption process or had been unsuccessful in doing so. In many cases social workers were able to answer only a few of the questions about the circumstances of the birthfather (Neil, 2000, p. 310).

Neil refers to as 'a wider pattern of the non-involvement of fathers with the adopted children in this study', draws attention to social workers' failure to enquire about the birth father and concludes that 'should some of the children in this sample need to know about their father to complete their sense of identity, disappointment is likely' (Neil, 2000, p. 314). Ten years later, Roskill found that there was no information recorded about birth fathers in 20% of the cases in her study of child protection cases (Roskill, 2011). The figure was higher, at 31% for the fathers of children who were in care. In *fostering* services the picture appears worse, a USA study of 1,222 caseworkers found that the service had failed to contact the non-resident father in almost 50% of cases in which children were placed in care (Malm *et al.*, 2006).

The work of the London-based agency Family Rights Group (FRG) has been important in highlighting fathers' exclusion in *child protection*. The FRG has consistently drawn attention to lack of details of father and paternal networks in social work records, failure to include non-resident fathers in child protection proceedings and schools that do not recognise the non-resident father when it comes to distribution of school reports, notices of parent evenings etc. In Ryan's (2000) study of UK child protection practices, she finds that fathers were minimally involved. A more recent Canadian study of child protection practice found that social workers considered almost 50% of fathers irrelevant to both mothers and children (Strega *et al.*, 2008). In Baynes and Holland's (2012) study of forty child protection case files, more than a third of fathers had no contact with a social worker prior to the first child protection meeting. Roskill's (2011) audit of cases involving domestically violent men found that fathers were neither seen nor contacted by phone in 32% of the core assessments studied. The upshot is that social workers' knowledge upon which to base a thorough risk and resource assessment is flawed.

In relation to youth offending, Harper and McLanahan (2004) found that adolescents in households in which the father was not present faced greater risk of imprisonment, and Page *et al.* note that: 'courts were seen as not adequately ensuring that fathers were present whenever possible … (even where the father was resident or active in their child's life) (Page *et al.*, 2008, p. 7).

Whether as a risk or an asset, fathers have been overlooked in child protection. In their study, Ferguson and Hogan (2004) observe that:

> some men contribute to their exclusion by refusing to seek or accept help. But others, despite being labelled dangerous

> men, were never known to have actually been violent. They were excluded simply on the basis of stories, appearances, perceptions (Ferguson and Hogan, 2004, p. 8).

They conclude that: 'the most troubling examples of exclusion we came across involved the systematic discarding of men as fathers without even the minimum of engagement, such as a conversation with him' (Ferguson and Hogan, 2004, p. 155).

This brings us to the next discussion, which will suggest that lack of inclusion is only one dynamic in the failure to engage fathers. As we will see, an equally powerful detractor is that of attitudes towards fathers.

Negativity and bias, distrust and hostility

This section concentrates on the barriers to father-inclusive practice and asks questions of how social workers regard the contribution of fathers to the welfare of their children because:

> While most service provision seeks to maintain and improve mother–child relationships even when mothers are highly vulnerable (Ashley *et al.*, 2006; Scott and Crooks, 2004), practitioners and policymakers usually approach father–child relationships at best casually and at worst with hostility (Family Commission, 2009, p. 31).

Is such negativity and hostility widespread?

In their study of social worker attitudes, Hawkins and Dollahite (1997) found unexamined negative generalisations (prejudices) about men/fathers to be widespread. These can include such beliefs as:

- men are unable to change;
- men are not willing to change;
- a man cannot cope with children without a woman to help him;
- fathers do not love their children as much as mothers do.

Russell *et al.* (1999) found service providers unsure about fathers' (men's) capacity to understand children's changing needs, or provide them with care and emotional support – with a substantial minority holding wildly exaggerated notions of the prevalence of father–daughter sexual abuse.

A US study of child protection practitioner attitudes revealed participants' beliefs that 'it was easier to work with families made up of single mothers and children.' The accounts continued:

> One worker with 24 years of experience stated flatly: 'We don't involve fathers. The system is mother focused.' Another worker said, 'If the mother says the father is dead, we stop right there. It quite simply is easier than trying to locate the father, especially if we feel the mom will not be cooperative.' Yet another worker made the point, 'A father in the family makes it harder. It's easier to let dad stay in the background and not deal with him. Then I don't have to deal with my own issues about men. It is easier to deal with mom only' (National Child Welfare Resources Center for Family-Centered Practice, 2002).

Another USA study echoed the last viewpoint when it found that 44% of case workers answered in the affirmative that 'involving non-resident fathers makes a case more complicated' (Malm *et al.*, 2006). I will return to the belief that child protection is 'easier' when social workers engage with 'mom only'.

Scourfield in his study of a child protection team in Wales notes that 'hopeless' men can be the butt of office humour and irreverent comment (Scourfield, 2001, p. 82) and found that both men and women child protection workers held negative opinions of men born from 'a deep-rooted legacy of men not being considered the business of child protection workers' (Scourfield, 2006, p. 441). Researchers in the USA concluded that:

> Worker bias regarding father involvement appears to be the most widely researched barrier to fathers' participation in child welfare case planning. One study found that caseworkers did not pay attention to birth fathers to the degree that they did to birth mothers. Worker bias regarding father involvement appears to be the most widely researched barrier to fathers' participation in child welfare case planning (Rosenberg and Wilcox, 2006, p. 25).

Dominelli and colleagues researched the attitudes of child protection workers in Canada over a number of years and observe that 'the child protection gaze remains firmly fixed on the mother' (Strega *et al.*, 2008, p. 706). In their most recent study they conclude that 'social workers do not completely trust fathers to care for children' (Dominelli *et al.*, 2011, p. 364).

In the UK, Page *et al.* in their review of services for fathers undertaken on behalf of the Department for Children, Schools and Families (DCSF) found that:

> there was also some evidence from interviewees that 'traditional' views of fathers remained prevalent among the workforce. This was seen to have led some staff to hold negative attitudes towards males as less able or willing carers of young children (particularly in Sure Start Children's Centres and safeguarding and looked after children) (Page *et al.*, 2008, p. 89).

Negativity and bias, distrust and hostility. What are the reasons for such prejudicial attitudes and practices? There is much speculation, Ferguson and Hogan wonder whether it is something in 'the very nature of social work' (Ferguson and Hogan, 2004, p. 9). Others suggest an over-dominance of a strand of feminist thinking that trivialises fathers (Young and Nathanson, 2012), while others point to the predominance of women in social work (Page *et al.*, 2008) with the concomitant suggestion that a female social worker's fear of male violence underpins a reluctance to engage with fathers (Carson, 2011). In the same vein, others, as indicated in the above quote from the USA child protection worker, suggest that if women practitioners had had the opportunity to explore their feelings and experiences relating to fathers and men there may not be as much reluctance to engage with fathers (Daniel and Taylor, 2001).

More structural reasons have been advanced including social work's roots in the welfare state with its emphasis on father as breadwinner and mother as homemaker (Christie, 2001). Elsewhere I have drawn attention to social work's other roots in 1940s' and 1950s' psychiatry and psychology and to child development theorists such as John Bowlby who have laid the basis for deep-seated social work beliefs in a centrality of mothers that marginalises fathers (Clapton, 2009). Silverstein and Auerbach suggest that Bowlby's research 'essentialised' mothers (Silverstein and Auerbach, 1999, p. 67) with the consequence that such influential figures in the development of social work, children and family thinking have downgraded fathers. The same can be said of many of the other writers who remain an influence on social work such as Carl Rogers, Abraham Maslow and Erik Erikson.

Thus, despite the rhetoric of increased father involvement and in the face of other services making changes (e.g. maternity services) to include fathers, in the words of Brown *et al.*: 'The idea that it is "cool" to be a dad has not yet penetrated child welfare thinking' (Brown *et al.*, 2009, p. 25). Also, child protection services remain:

> founded on the notion that it is the central task of social workers to break the cycle of child maltreatment by successfully teaching mothers how to do their job properly, or removing children from a home where that is impossible' (Brown *et al.*, 2009, p. 29).

Policymaking: Absence and imagery

Another driver that marginalises and serves to denigrate fathers is the activities of policymakers, trainers and child protection experts. In my discussion of how fathers are written about and portrayed I cite examples from child protection research, writing, policy and training to show a pervasiveness of negative attitudes towards fathers. These range from a straightforward failure to include fathers in the picture, sometimes literally, to more disturbing rendering of every father in every case example or scenario as invisible, abusive or useless. There remain numerous examples of this (Clapton, 2009). Two examples will suffice, but many more can be found.

The first, it is suggested, is indicative of the countless case scenarios that are generated throughout child protection training. The following extracts are taken from training materials produced for the Children's Workforce Development Council (CWDC). The first of these is a list of scenarios for discussion:

- Alex (aged seventeen) moved to the area six months ago with her mother, to be nearer her grandparents. She has struggled with the move but does attend college where she is on a vocational course.

- Sam (aged three) has mild hearing loss and some communication difficulties. There are some issues around his behaviour and social skills at nursery … Both parents are getting very tired of the whole situation and taking their frustrations out on Katy, the health visitor.
- Lettia is seventeen and is currently six months pregnant. Ever since she had her pregnancy confirmed her attendance at college has started to be very sporadic. Prior to the pregnancy she was predicted good grades at A level. Lettia feels that one of the reasons her attendance has slipped is due to her feeling uncertain about the future. She lacks support from her father, who does not even talk to her and does not want her in the house once the baby is born. Her mother is more supportive, but the situation has caused arguments at home. Lettia wants the baby but does not want to live in the current atmosphere.
- The father of the baby (aged nineteen) has disappeared, and friends have told Lettia he has moved away, which has left Lettia feeling very alone.
- John is six and his performance at school has dropped significantly over the last term, since his move to a new school. He finds it difficult to concentrate and fit into an ordered and structured school environment. John has also been refusing to go to school as least once a week, and his parents have struggled to get him there. His parents are worried that this may be linked to some form of bullying … John's mother is at her wits' end and is completely unsure of what to do next. John will talk to her about some things, but starts shouting and screaming if he is asked about school. John's mum is desperate to get help from someone but is not happy with the school as she feels they could do more to help. There have been discussions with John's teacher, but both parents have felt that they were being blamed for lack of attendance (CWDC, 2010, p. 12).

The second extract continues in the above vein of father absence and mother responsibility and concerns the case of the last child, John (CWDC, 2010, p. 18). A casework plan is suggested in Table 2.1.

Table 2.1: A casework plan for John

John			
Person	**Advantages**	**Disadvantages**	**Choose as lead professional?**
John's mum	knows John well	wants support from practitioners	not a good choice in this case
Education welfare	can support main needs and initiated the CAF [common assessment framework] with consent from parents and gets on with John	relationship with parents could be better	a good choice as the relationship with Mum and John was good enough to undertake CAF and hits most of the other criteria
Learning mentor	can support main needs and has potential for a positive relationship with parents	does not know the area yet	could be a good choice with support to understand local provision
Family support worker	Mum has chosen to involve them so probably a positive relationship	new to the situation and focused on supporting Mum	not a good choice here – useful to involve, but not focused specifically on John

Source: Children's Workforce Development Council, 2010, p. 15.

It is suggested that the lack of any positive father involvement in the above CWDC training materials will be found in the vast majority training materials used up and down the UK.

The second way that messages are conveyed about fathers and families is images that do not include men. The most recent Scottish child protection guidelines (Scottish Government, 2010) were issued with a front cover that pictured a woman and two children (Figure 2.1).

Rendering fathers out of the picture is not confined to official documents. Quarriers, a Scottish charity, ran a series of advertisements in 2012, one of which enjoined the viewer to 'think family' and was accompanied by a mother and baby (Figure 2.2).

The prevalence of such father-free images of families is such that, unless one's antenna is up, they can pass by without remark. They also feed into a certain collective consciousness especially regarding families in need. Equally when fathers are shown as layabouts and/or threatening, this too, in the absence of any balance, sends out a message to be both wary and suspicious of fathers. The 2012 campaign

Figure 2.1: *National Guidance for Child Protection in Scotland* cover.

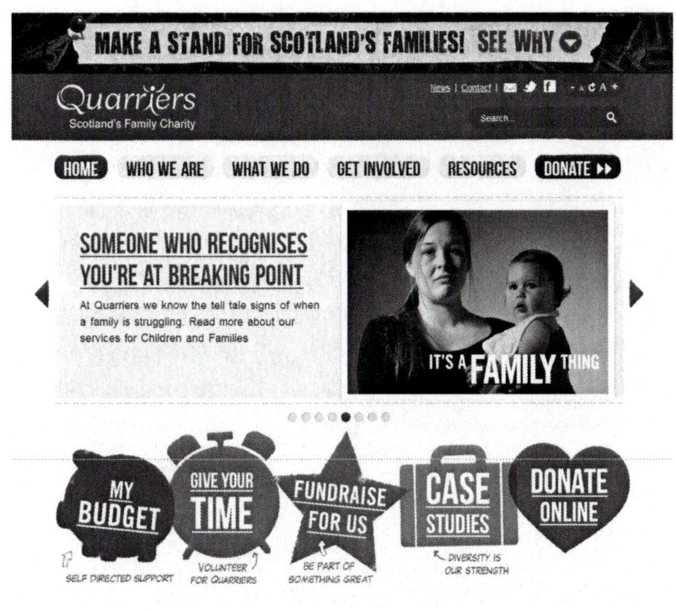

Figure 2.2: Quarriers website screengrab

Figure 2.3: Children's Panel screengrab.

to recruit panel members for the Scottish Children's Hearings is an example of this (Figure 2.3).

In order to influence practice and agencies in the field, policymakers must set an example by being more inclusive of fathers in their statements and images, and training should use scenarios and examples that take a more even-handed approach to the depiction of fathers and their behaviours.

The next chapters are less concerned with naming the obstacles and barriers. Instead, they concentrate on developing positive practice with fathers and their families, beginning with how to reach and engage fathers.

Key research and resources

Evaluating the Evidence: Fathers, Families and Children, National Academy for Parenting Research (2010). Available at URL: www.iop.kcl.ac.uk/iopweb/blob/downloads/locator/l_1119_Fathers,_families_and_children.pdf (accessed 17 December 2012)

The Costs and Benefits of Active Fatherhood, Fathers Direct (2008). Available at URL: www.fatherhoodinstitute.org/2008/fatherhood-institute-main-research-summary-the-costs-and-benefits-of-active-fatherhood (accessed 17 December 2012)

Fatherhood Institute Research Summary: Fathers' Impact on Their Children's Learning and Achievement, Fatherhood Institute (2010). Available at URL: www.fatherhoodinstitute.org/2010/fatherhood-institute-research-summary-fathers-and-their-childrens-education (accessed 17 December 2012)

CHAPTER 3

Reaching and Engaging Fathers

CASE STUDY – THE 'A' FAMILY

This case analysis involves a family of three, known as the A family – a mother, aged twenty-four and her two daughters aged ten and six. The family live in a deprived area of the city. The mother does not work, and the family survives on state benefits. The mother suffers from depression and inconsistently uses Prozac to help stabilise her fluctuating moods. Neither child had involvement with their father or any other extended family. The only close family that is available for support is the mother's older sister who also lives locally; however, this relationship is turbulent and inconsistent.

The above description is taken from a final year social work student's dissertation with identifying details altered. In discussion of the draft dissertation, the student was asked about the father's whereabouts and circumstances. In another relationship? Prison? Dead? The student was asked to enquire and the message came back: 'He's out of the picture.' It was agreed that the student raise this in their next visit with the mother, and when they did so the mother said that he lived around the corner 'BUT was a waste of space.' The discussion that ensued established that:

- the father was alive and nearby, that his parents were also alive;
- the daughters held memories of him and his parenting and knew of him via local community connections;
- the daughters regularly had to dissemble when the subject of fathers came up in school;
- while the father was never discussed in the house, the

> daughters had talked between themselves about him and his second family.

It is understood that not all persistence will reveal details of fathers as in the above account; however, the passing reference to the father will be very familiar to students, tutors, practice teachers and social workers. And, as we have seen, in many instances case notes etc. do not mention him at all. Once the above father's whereabouts and his and his family's place in the lives of the children were broached, the next task was to continue the conversation with the mother about their value.

Before positive practice is discussed, however, it seems essential at this point in the book to pause and state the obvious. The value of fathers has been outlined, and the neglect of and bias concerning fathers explored. (Practices at team and agency level and training and education will be explored later.) If one of the major barriers to developing positive practice with fathers is attitude, then it follows that, unless practitioners are signed up to an appreciation of the value of involved fathering, then no amount of evidence plus tips and hints will be successful. Practitioners can make a huge difference in their day-to-day work with children and families. But without a *belief* – at an individual level – in the value to women, children and families of engaging fathers, then no amount of facts will bring about change.

Believing in fathering

For successful engagement, fathers must be recognised as equal to mothers in their parental roles and responsibilities. In their survey of the generic barriers to engaging with fathers, Page *et al.* comment that 'some staff in family services did not view engagement with fathers as a priority and did not think proactive support was important to engage fathers' (Page *et al.*, 2008, p. 7).

Research undertaken by the FRG concluded that workers must have positive attitudes towards working with fathers (Ashley *et al.*, 2006) and findings from 162 parent support professionals from twelve local authorities found that the ways in which fathers were approached about engagement had a direct effect on their involvement (Cullen *et al.*, 2010). Ultimately, workers must appreciate that:

> Children, mothers and fathers suffer when workers fail to engage purposefully with fathers and father-figures. To move toward true inclusiveness in both protecting and supporting children, practitioners need to proactively assess and engage with all significant men in a child's life, understanding that some may pose risks, some may be assets and some may incorporate aspects of both (Strega *et al.*, 2008, p. 713).

Positive practice with fathers will be hampered without a belief that fathers are significant and can be a force for good in the lives of women and children. Furthermore, if workers proceed on the assumption that fathers will want to engage, then this is a factor in engaging fathers. As previously noted, it is acknowledged that the behaviour of some fathers will work against the development of a positive attitude. In the words of Ferguson:

> It seems that as they go about their day-to-day work and approach the homes of service users, one of the things that most fills practitioners with anxiety and even dread is that there may be a man behind the door (Ferguson, 2011, p. 151).

This book does not dismiss such feelings of dread and has already drawn attention to some of the reasons that may underpin this. These may be based on assumptions and be unrelated to any actual evidence of risk. However, some men are violent and do pose a risk to families and sometimes, but much less often, to professionals engaged with the family. Chapter 5 looks more closely at working with fathers who are deemed to be a risk.

Finding fathers

Research tells us that early work to find, contact and involve fathers lays the basis for their greater engagement (Garbers *et al.*, 2006). Burgess remarks: 'Much of the "invisible father" syndrome arises from workers simply not "seeing" fathers who are present in households – no data collected, not invited, no pressure, if they don't attend meetings' (Burgess, 2005, p. 68). Positive practice with fathers signals that they are important and expected to be involved from the outset. A USA project to improve father involvement found that: 'when fathers are located and identified as a resource, there are incremental increases over time in fathers' involvement in case planning and the fathers' extended family involvement in case planning' (English *et al.*, 2009, p. 233). Other research (on non-resident fathers) has shown success in engaging fathers follows workers identifying, locating and contacting them within thirty days after case opening (Malm *et al.*, 2006).

There is generally always a father or father-figure in the picture. A US study of families receiving services from child welfare found that a majority of primary caregivers (88%) reported some form of male relative involvement, whether that included a relationship by caregiver status, marriage, household membership or contact with a non-custodial biological parent (Bellamy, 2009).

Workers should not conclude that a non-resident father has written himself out of the child's life. As a matter of routine, the initial referral process ought to record both parents' details. Most successful information-gathering about the identity and location of a non-resident father occurs very early in the case as part of investigation or assessment. If a non-resident father's identity and location are not determined early on, there is less of a chance the agency will successfully engage at a later stage (Malm *et al.*, 2006). Whether a father is non-resident or not, services that refuse to accept referrals without mention of or information about the father will tend to have higher levels of father engagement (Fabiano, 2007).

The 'basics' of father engagement require consideration regarding the timing of any meetings or other services to enable the attendance of fathers who are at work. Many services remain run on a 9–5, five days a week basis. Bayley *et al.* (2009) recommend flexibility of provision because while 9–5 weekday hours are difficult for some, so too can evenings and weekends be difficult for others, because of work commitments.

Communication with both parents should be standard practice. Non-resident fathers should receive notice of any meeting to which they are invited at the same time as the mother or other resident carer. Hearing from a child, or from the mother, or other relative about a meeting marginalises the importance of the father and makes engagement less likely. Attention ought also to be paid to the particular position of non-resident fathers who will be travelling from another, perhaps further away, location (Huebner *et al.*, 2008). As regards communication, implicit messages can be conveyed about who is welcome and who is thought superfluous. Page *et al.* found that:

> fathers were seen to be less likely than mothers to respond to communication (including any marketing as well as direct communication with parents) that was not addressed to them, did not refer directly to fathers or did not include positive images of fathers and their children (Page *et al.*, 2008, p. 7).

Page *et al.* also draw attention to the practice of recording only the home address for the child, thus omitting additional addresses for non-resident parents, even where both mother and father had requested that their separate addresses be recorded and used (Page *et al.*, 2008, p. 88). Although this is time-consuming, research tells us that the most successful work with children and families involves both parents (Bakermans-Kranenburg *et al.*, 2003).

For fathers of children involved in child protection processes, working with non-statutory agencies can provide alternative locations for provision and facilitate engagement with fathers who might be unwilling to engage with local authority services (Page *et al.*, 2008).

Finding fathers: Mothers and 'gatekeeping'

> Research consistently suggests that the single most powerful predictor of a father's involvement with his children is the quality of his relationship with their mother, regardless of whether the couple is married, divorced, separated or never-married. A father who gets along well with his children's mother is more likely to take an active interest in his children's upbringing. This finding, coupled with the fact that most mothers take the role of 'lead parent' in managing their children's time, suggests that mothers may be the best route for getting fathers involved in children's services (Asmussen and Weizel, 2010, p. 9).

The research seems unanimous here. Mothers are central. Where the father is reported as not being in the picture and whether or not he is resident with the family, the mother's encouragement of his involvement, or at least decision not to oppose, is crucial. Scourfield *et al.* draw upon US-based research to note that:

> Mothers can either facilitate or block access for both resident and non-resident fathers (Huebner *et al.*, 2008; O'Donnell *et al.*, 2005). In their study of 1,958 US cases, Malm *et al.* (2006) found that only one third of mothers identified the father when asked (Scourfield *et al.*, 2011, p. 12).

They go on to outline some of the reasons for this. These include:

> reluctance about letting the father know that child welfare services are involved, fear that the father may gain custody, anger at the father for being in a new relationship or fear of the father's reaction, particularly if there has been a history of domestic abuse (Scourfield *et al.*, 2011).

Scourfield *et al.* then note a financial disincentive: 'a mother may receive more money informally from the father or assume she qualifies for more welfare benefits if his presence in the home is not known' (Scourfield *et al.*, 2011). The varied reasons for disavowing the presence of a father are clearly a matter for sensitive negotiation that starts with the best interests of both child and mother.

While Featherstone criticises the notion of mothers as gatekeepers as problematic, because it assumes that mothers need to have the importance of fathers explained to them (Featherstone, 2010, p. 185), the research seems unanimous. Mothers have a pivotal role in facilitating, or not, father involvement. The mother in this chapter's opening case study will require to trust someone who can offer reassurance that she or her children will not be at risk of harm should she be convinced of the father's and his family's value to her daughters.

The degree of animosity between ex-partners cannot be ignored; however, ways through this can be found. The mother in this chapter's opening case made known the father's mobile phone number to the student, who then offered to chaperone at a meeting and outing for the daughters and their father. This went well, and after more shuttle-diplomacy the daughters were able to go for an overnight stay, thus providing the mother with a break.

Male or female worker?

It is accepted that there is a predominance of females in family services and social work (Page *et al.*, 2008), especially at practice level, and that there needs to be more men employed at this level in childcare in general (Bayley *et al.*, 2009). Furthermore, it is also agreed that childcare services 'face' women and mothers more than they do fathers. The range of childcare centre services offered to parents, for example, generally appeals to women, images on posters, magazines in waiting rooms – even colour schemes – all combine to dissuade men from lingering any further after they have dropped off their child. However, the discussion about who is best to engage fathers has not arrived at a consensus. The view of Velazquez and Vincent is typical of one of two main positions: '... when interacting with male caseworkers, fathers are less defensive because they are not as preoccupied with being perceived negatively or treated unfairly' (Velazquez and Vincent, 2009, p. 9). This has been echoed in a UK study that emphasises the value of male workers:

> ... at the point of fathers accessing and engaging with services. Male workers had taken lead roles in consultation with fathers and in developing accessible service models, particularly in children's centres. Staff consulted believed strongly in the value of a balanced workforce, with positive attitudes about the roles of both mothers and fathers (Gilligan *et al.*, 2012, p. 13).

The influential UK Fatherhood Institute tends to agree:

> Fathers tend to prefer one-on-one interventions to groups, and may be more willing to attend mixed-sex groups than 'fathers' groups', although attendees at male- only groups often value the single-sex environment. In some settings (e.g. antenatal), mixed-sex groups may usefully divide into single-sex groups for individual sessions (Fatherhood Institute, 2009a, pp. 4–5).

However, the Fatherhood Institute goes on to note that 'Fathers' groups should always be regarded as only one among a range of ways for engaging with fathers' (Fatherhood Institute, 2009a).

Some research suggests that the gender of the practitioner is not as important as attitude and that men work well with male or female practitioners when they can develop a positive working alliance with them (Bowman *et al.*, 2001; Featherstone, 2004).

Excluding (some) fathers

Not all fathers will want to be found; however, even those men need to be offered the opportunity to step up. There will be other fathers for whom there is compelling evidence to indicate their exclusion, even at an early stage. In cases such as these, Ferguson and Hogan call for distinctions to be made:

> between avoiding the man *per se* in awkwardly trying to pretend (or wish) that he wasn't there, and excluding him from work with the family because it is viewed as better for them if he is not included in their lives. In the latter scenario, the man is consciously and openly excluded from 'family work' and rationales given for this, as it is viewed as being in the best interests of the children, and partner (Ferguson and Hogan, 2004, p. 32).

The question of how to develop positive practice with fathers who are deemed or thought to be a risk is returned to in Chapter 5. However, it ought to be noted that social workers need to make every effort to engage with fathers' versions of events in as non-accusatory manner as possible (Roskill *et al.*, 2008).

Engaging with fathers: What do you say after you say 'hello'?

Many of the issues facing fathers as they try to be good parents are the same as those facing mothers – stress, finances, limited time, to name a few. How fathers perceive and react to these is usually different and is often grounded in cultural views and expectations of manhood and fatherhood.

First contact between a father and a worker is a unique opportunity to establish the basis for a positive strengths-based relationship free of commonly identified negative assumptions. A meaningful first contact can set the stage for frequent, ongoing, high-quality interactions that ultimately benefit the child. Whether or not that worker is able to make a 'heart-to-heart' connection by demonstrating empathy, understanding and belief in the father's potential can greatly influence a father's decision to get involved.

Key factors for initial engagement will vary for different fathers, but may include the following:

- a comfortable relationship with an enthusiastic, caring worker whom fathers trust and who responds to their needs;
- service within their 'comfort zone' and relevant to their own concerns.

Men may find 'talking about feelings or problems' off-putting at first as well as services defined as 'offering help' rather than engaging with the men as a resource in children's lives.

Another common scenario is that, even when a father is present in the home during an initial contact or home visit, there may be a tendency for him to absent himself from the room or let his partner do all the talking. In their analysis of serious case reviews, Brandon *et al.* refer to health workers who 'were aware of the father being very much in the background and not participating. Rather he was an onlooker standing in a darker part of the room' (Brandon *et al.*, 2009, pp. 51–2). Rivett notes:

> In the detailed description of the interventions used by Haringey staff much was made of the work with Baby P's mother to improve her parenting skills, but little effort was made to engage the men in the household either in treatment or in assessment of the risk to Baby P. No clearer example is needed to emphasise that child welfare workers – from all professions, need to have a greater understanding of the assessment and treatment of violent male carers, whether they are fathers, stepfathers or partners (Rivett, 2010, p. 196).

This is an opportunity for positive practice with fathers, possible father-figures by acknowledging them, bringing them out of the 'darker part of the room', enquiring about their concerns and eliciting their strengths and assessing their shortcomings. Men should not be allowed to leave the room with a wave of the hand to signal a woman-only discussion about women's issues (i.e. child welfare and protection). Skills involved here are considerable, and with certain categories of men (e.g. young fathers) the best will in the world may not prevent the father deferring to or passing responsibility to the mother and switching off. It may be that, in cases such as this, two workers are necessary or at the very least, one-on-one time devoted to the father. What is certain is that, if a worker tacitly or otherwise accepts the non-involvement of the father, this will only strengthen the view that a father's engagement is not necessary and not wanted.

To conclude, positive practice in reaching and engaging fathers is basic good practice, and includes assumption of good faith, clarity about the purpose of contact, and an unprejudiced and non-judgemental attitude. The next chapter looks at good practice once a father is engaged.

Best practice points in reaching and engaging fathers

- Understand how important fathers are in the lives of their children;
- genuinely respect and care about men and women equally;
- encourage to mothers to trust that involving the fathers will be to their advantage;
- respect fathers for sometimes being different from mothers and having different priorities and ways of doing things;
- start where the father is, not where you think he should be;
- work from the premise that fathers love their children deeply and that negative behaviour or expressions of feeling may be defensive responses, which can be worked through;
- recognise that most fathers will do anything for their children, but may need to be helped to understand their children's needs;
- understand that fathers are the real experts on their own support needs;
- help a father to see the 'evidence' of a problem (e.g. sharing information and assessment results) so he is encouraged to take part in services;
- be prepared to hang in there with fathers who may have reasons not to engage;

- be supportive, but also hold fathers accountable;
- build on small successes.

Key research and resources

Fathers Matter: Research Findings on Fathers and Their Involvement with Social Care services (2006), The Family Rights Group. Available from URL: www.frg.org.uk (accessed 17 December 2012)

Strengthening Families Through Fathers: Developing Policy and Practice in Relation to Vulnerable Fathers and Their Families, H. Ferguson and F. Hogan (2004), especially Chapter 4. Available at URL: http://repository.wit.ie/676/1/foreword.pdf (accessed 17 December 2012)

CHAPTER 4

Working with Fathers

What are the principles for positive practice with fathers?

Fathers come in all shapes, sizes and categories (e.g. young fathers, non-resident fathers, birth fathers and adoptive fathers) and often the categories overlap as in the case of young fathers who do not or cannot live with the child and its mother. For this reason, it has proved impossible to devise typical case scenarios for this book. This chapter outlines good practice with the key categories of fathers that are likely to be involved with social services. It begins, however, with what the literature tells us is constructive and successful practice with all fathers.

As a caution to those who approach the issue as one of promoting or maintaining relationships between fathers and their children, Featherstone (2009) observes that fathers must be located in the broader familial context, that is, practice that ignores the mother, her sensitivities and concerns is unlikely to bring about change for the good. The mother's relations with, and views and feelings about, the father must be understood, addressed and discussed, but not necessarily be the only or primary consideration. Ultimately, as noted in the previous chapter on mother's 'gatekeeping', support or at least understanding from the mother is a vital element in maintenance and development of child–father relations. Furthermore, respectful relations between parents are predictors of the best outcomes for children.

In 2008 the UK government's Think Family initiative recognised the limitations of work with just one parent and emphasised that the optimum approach was that of engaging with both parents. A meta-analysis of interventions aiming to enhance positive parental behaviours has found that those involving fathers appear to be significantly more effective than interventions focusing on mothers only. Interestingly, the study found that interventions that involve fathers as well as mothers seem to be more effective in enhancing *each* parent's sensitivity to their child, and their child's attachment to them (Bakermans-Kranenburg *et al.*, 2003). Lundahl *et al.*'s (2008) meta-analysis of parent training evaluations similarly found that programmes involving both mothers and fathers achieved more desirable parenting practices and more positive changes in children's behaviour than programmes involving only mothers.

However, bearing in mind, to rephrase Featherstone, the limitations of focusing solely on the father–child dyad, what are the main messages for the most successful work with fathers? Time and again it has been found that such work is infused with a strengths-based approach. Such an approach, as noted in the discussion on engaging fathers, believes in the value of fathering and the positive contribution men can make to their children's lives. Strengths-based practice involves workers who are positive about the father's ability, honest about the issues faced and build on his existing skills, using solution-focused thinking to develop these and build his confidence (Berlyn *et al.*, 2008). Bartlett and Vann (2004) suggest that the key factors for ongoing engagement include:

- a strong ongoing relationship with a worker and/or other service users;
- feeling valued;
- a sense of 'team' and 'ownership';
- real changes in their family relationships and other areas of their lives;
- services that address the concerns that may have led fathers to join the project and that help them move towards their goals in practical ways.

The opposite of a strengths-based approach is that of one driven by deficit assumptions. Such assumptions create little change in fathers because they:

- have little recognition of growth and development;

- misconstrue the motives, feelings, attitudes and hopes of most fathers;
- create barriers to change rather than its promotion;
- have a narrow standard of good parenting (from Hawkins and Dollahite, 1997).

Strengths-based work

What does a strength-based approach look like? Ferguson and Hogan argue that practitioners should strive to:

> 'join with' men and invite them to become more than they were ever told they could be, realising that any such change in fathers will also necessitate a change in the family and social system too and supporting that developmental process (Ferguson and Hogan, 2004, p. 175).

They go on to suggest a conversation model of work that avoids an air of professional suspicion and accusation, which leads only to defensiveness and disengagement. Instead:

> The trick is to confront the man about any relevant concerns and render him accountable in the context of building up a broad picture of how he sees his life and himself as a father. The man needs to get the message very quickly that the professional is not there simply to talk with and about him as a problem, but has a much broader interest in him as a man and father (Ferguson and Hogan, pp. 177–8).

RECONNECTING MEN WITH THEIR OWN CHILDHOOD

Many writers argue that fathers who need help are fathers who need to talk about their own experiences of being fathered (Daniel and Taylor, 2001).

Ferguson and Hogan (2004, pp. 179–80) suggest the following questions as part of such work:

- Where did you get the ideas about the type of father you know you want to be?
- Who taught you most about being a father?
- Where do you find your supports for being the type of father you are?
- What type of man was your own father?
- What type of things did he do in the family?
- How would you describe your relationship together?
- Are there things he did that you would want to make sure to do as a father now?

- Are there things he did that you really do not want to carry on doing?
- What have you learnt about being a father from your mother?
- Who else do you believe has taught you about being a dad?
- What have your children taught you?
- What advice or expertise would you pass on to a new father?

See also G. Clapton (2003b) *How Do You Remember Your Father? How Will Your Children Remember You?*, a report on successful work with fathers in Scottish prisons

A man ought to be given early opportunities to say positive things about how he views himself as a father. Ferguson and Hogan argue that:

> this gives him the message that you are interested in all sides of him, and in helping him to develop what he feels he does well so that he can do it as often as possible (Ferguson and Hogan, 2004, p. 178).

At an individual level, a practitioner's experience with, and assumptions about, men and fathers will impact on their capacity to work with them from a strengths-based perspective. Practitioners must want to work with men. Having a healthy view of the capabilities of men to build relationships is fundamental. Previous chapters have discussed attitudes essential for reaching and engaging with fathers; once engaged, the most productive *attitudes* include recognising that men have the ability to:

- commit to the physical and ongoing support that a father provides and their involvement with their children throughout their lives;
- make day-to-day decisions that meet the needs of their children;
- work as an active and effective member of a 'parenting team';
- care about and attend to the important transitions in a child's life, and work to provide the optimal conditions to maximise their growth;
- create resources for material well-being and resolve problems in ways that promote emotional well-being;
- form lasting and healthy attachments with their children and learn to adapt and change as their children grow;

- relate with children by sharing meaningfully with them, both verbally and non-verbally (Australian Fatherhood Research Network, 2009, pp. 46–7).

What of the *skills* required for a strengths-based approach with fathers? These will include the ability to:

- model effective, respectful and inclusive communication (including verbal and non-verbal communication, listening, empathic responding, non-judgemental paraphrasing, summarising, questioning, effective conflict resolution, assertiveness, use of humour, tact and sensitivity) when working with fathers;
- value and work inclusively with them while considering the full range of possible influences in their lives (including personality, culture, language, religion, age, gender, family of origin, education levels, learning abilities, economic situation, social context, health, disabilities and related issues) and the impact of how these interrelate.

An obvious point, given that fathers are regularly overlooked, is that any strength-based approach will be skilled at the little things, such as sharing information otherwise unavailable to fathers. Other 'little things' may include going the extra mile: for example, telephone contact at the weekends. De Boer and Cody outline a useful comprehensive list of what works in building successful relationships; this includes 'going the extra mile in fulfilling mandated responsibilities, stretching professional mandates and boundaries' (De Boer and Cody, 2007, p. 35). Such little things are important actions for all, but especially count in rapport-building with fathers.

As indicated in the introduction to this chapter, there are many categories of fathers. There now follows some key insights and practice points that relate to specific groups of fathers, especially those likely to be involved with child welfare and protection agencies.

Young fathers

Young fathers face the challenges that all fathers face as regards their relative exclusion from childcare, and on top of this they are often stereotyped as being especially irresponsible and uncaring. Kiselica argues that:

> For too long, our culture has treated boys who become fathers ... as detached misfits who are the architects of many of our nation's problems, rather than seeing these youth for who they really are: young men trying to navigate a complex array of difficult life circumstances that place them at a tremendous disadvantage (Kiselica, 2008, p. 195).

Young mothers do not have it easy. However:

> Although some teenage mothers may often feel 'blamed' by society at large, they are clearly established as stakeholders with a legitimate claim on services. The same does not hold true for teenage fathers (Gilligan *et al.*, 2012, p. 1).

What we know now is that fatherhood can be a 'wake-up call' for many disadvantaged young men, with early fatherhood providing a trigger to growing maturity, expressed in aspirations of 'being there' for their child and social responsibility. Young fathers fallen foul of the criminal justice system see fatherhood as an important motivator for change. A study of eighteen- to twenty-year-old male offenders – 30% of whom were fathers or had a pregnant partner or ex-partner – identified six factors that would contribute to successful resettlement. These were:

- gaining employment;
- having stable housing;
- being in a relationship;
- having a child;
- having positive family relations;
- managing drug/alcohol use (Farrant, 2006).

Farrant's study also revealed the post-release reality in which 75% of the young men interviewed had left home, and one in five was homeless. Many were living on the floors of friends or girlfriends on release from prison and had to keep moving. In such circumstances, it is easy to see how those who are fathers become estranged from their children.

The literature on fathers-to-be talks of a 'golden moment' in the process of becoming a father when feelings of paternity and selflessness kick in. Men's caring energy and desire for connection as a father increases dramatically around the time of the birth

(McKeowen *et al.*, 1998). And research tells us that four out of five births to teenage mothers are joint-registered with the father, that is, 80% of young partners are still close at the time of birth (Burgess, 2010). It is at this point then that services might make the most difference with young fathers-to-be, yet this is often an opportunity missed. Bunting (2005) found that, while health visitors estimated the needs of both teenage mothers and their partners as high, they would tend to expect the young mothers' parenting capacity to be average to good, and the young fathers' parenting capacity to be poor, and impute any decreases in couple/paternal contact to negative characteristics in the fathers. These assumptions were made despite the fact that the health visitors actually knew very little about the young fathers and were ill-equipped to offer them support, being neither aware of any support they might be receiving, nor of services that might be able to help them. Aside from public images and professional tendencies to overlook them, young fathers frequently face family rejection, barriers to contact with child and mother, a lack of means to contribute financially, and an inability to envision future achievements (Guterman and Lee, 2005). Other particular obstacles and challenges faced by and presented by young fathers include the following:

- They tend to believe they are unwelcome and inadequate as parents.
- They generally face lack of preparedness for fatherhood, cognitively and emotionally and their knowledge of infant development tends to be deficient and unrealistic.
- Many have difficulty controlling their tempers and express negative parenting attitudes and behaviours; related to this, they may be more likely than older fathers to be violent towards their partners and, possibly, their children.
- They need to reconcile the contradictory roles of adolescent and father and often to assume the responsibilities of adulthood before they are sufficiently mature.
- One US study found 47% of young fathers using alcohol, 40% having problems with the law and 42% having been in jail (Weinman *et al.*, 2005); other studies have identified higher than average involvement in drug use, although

most young fathers are not serious drug users (Guterman and Lee, 2005).

Young fathers also have very high rates of anxiety and depression. These are strongly correlated with younger age of onset of fatherhood, exposure to domestic violence as a child, and having no father alive (Quinlivan and Condon, 2005). Common mental health issues that young fathers report are related to relationships, neighbourhood, family, tobacco use, police and being a parent (Weinman *et al.*, 2005). Yet the young men's distress usually goes untreated: their formal contact with psychiatric services is no higher than that of older, less depressed fathers (Quinlivan and Condon, 2005), and they do not seem to recognise their own needs.

To make headway, workers need to appreciate that the vast majority of young fathers are keen to be, and stay, connected to their children. Young fathers have the same hopes to engage with their children as other fathers, and when this does not happen they are mainly anguished by that fact, with only a small percentage showing no joy about becoming fathers and having no intention of supporting their partner and children (Kiselica, 2008). Many young fathers claim that early fatherhood has given their lives meaning, as well as protecting them from involvement in a range of negative activities (Rouch, 2005).

So what should positive practice with young fathers consist of? The Fatherhood Institute suggests that young fathers tend to fall into one of three categories: 'chaotic', 'semi-chaotic' and 'sorted' (Fatherhood Institute, 2010b). All need support, but different strategies are required to engage effectively with these different kinds of young fathers.

Interventions that work with young fathers

What does not seem to work is group work. Sherriff (2007) found some practitioners operating groups for young fathers but reaching only a small minority that way, even though outcomes were positive for some individuals. Practitioners were also clear that group work is not appropriate for more chaotic young fathers; and that most young fathers need prior and continuing one-on-one engagement with professionals.

In addition to surmounting the attitudes and exclusionary practices of professionals, engaging with the gatekeeping role of mothers and their families and the mindsets of some young fathers themselves, what works best includes the following:

- Actively involving young fathers from the moment of pregnancy awareness, at the birth and in the early months and years of the child's life. This helps the men to take on a fatherhood identity from the start and live out their bond with the child through shared parenting, rather than trying to fit in around the mother's dominant role (Ferguson and Hogan, 2004).
- Krishnakumar and Black (2003) found that a young mother's satisfaction over time with the young father's involvement was predicted by a positive relationship between her own mother and the young man; they therefore recommend focus on role clarification for grandmothers and fathers as well as joint parenting activities for mothers and fathers, regardless of their romantic relationship.
- Because young fathers' access to their children is largely controlled by other people, interventions to support young men's fatherhood prove more productive when delivered in partnership with mothers, or at least with ongoing reference to them.
- Rather the young father being seen as, at best, an adjunct to the mother–child dyad, it is good practice to view him as a father *and* a young man with a need for one-on-one relationship that incorporates mentoring (Bronte-Tinkew *et al.*, 2008).
- A comprehensive array of services to young fathers which goes beyond parenting information alone, e.g. education and employment guidance.

Non-resident fathers

Before we begin this discussion it has to be acknowledged that it is harder, that is, more time-consuming, to deal with two separated parents than one, especially when the two are estranged from each other, but it is ultimately good practice for all concerned to do so.

Furthermore, the terminology ('non-resident') carries an air of condemnation; however, other terms are equally negative (e.g. separated parent). Therefore, bearing in mind the proviso that it is not the best phrase but is the most recognised, 'non-resident' will be used here.

Research undertaken for Gingerbread, the UK charity for one-parent families, found that the majority of children whose parents have separated continue to live with their mother and that the majority of parents (71%) reported face-to-face contact with the non-resident parent (Peacey and Hunt, 2009). Bradshaw *et al.*, (1999) found half of all absent fathers see their children once a week and the great majority of absent fathers were attempting to maintain relationships with their children. As mentioned previously, in most relationships the warmth and closeness of this contact is more significant than the frequency of the contact.

However, a significant minority (29%) of parents in the Gingerbread study reported no current contact, of which 63% of respondents claimed no contact whatsoever with the non-resident parent since separation. A further 6% said that the father was not aware of the child's existence (Peacey and Hunt, 2009, p. 17). There are, therefore, a considerable number of families in which contact is an issue, and in these cases it is more usually the non-resident father who does not have contact.

If, as we know, fathers living in families can be overlooked, then those fathers who do not live together with the mother and children are many times more liable to be excluded during assessments for services and interventions. This is not in the best interests of children. Notions of uninvolved or 'obstructive' parent mean that many non-resident fathers are absent from practitioner's minds and records and are thus anonymous. Such anonymity means that possibilities offered by the non-resident parent's family, culture and community are denied and unavailable to the child. Furthermore, psychological relationships among family members continue to exist following a separation or divorce, and an absent parent remains part of their children and their lives, despite periods of turmoil and loyalty conflicts. In Australia, Funder (1996) found 96% of children include their non-resident fathers as part of their families. Research on non-residence now tells us that *father-presence* is less concerned with residence and more interested in quality of relationships between all concerned (Johnson, 1996).

While not limited to fathers who do not live with their children, some writers have drawn special attention to the emotions expressed by men who live apart from them and how to engage with this. Ferguson and Hogan remark that:

> The striking thing about these men (those separated from their children by systems such as the courts) is their anger at the injustices they feel have been done to them. This is so manifest and 'in your face' that the real danger is that all professionals see is the angry, aggressive man and not the loving, caring father. Our experience in the research interviews attested to this. The importance of men feeling listened to and affirmed in themselves and in their struggles is a feature of every father we interviewed. But it takes on particular significance for those men who feel completely excluded by the system and whose relationships with their children are under threat because of the judgements of experts (Ferguson and Hogan, 2004, p. 67).

Positive practice with non-resident fathers will involve a mixture of listening, advocating and trust-building, especially if the worker is a social work professional and so social services have been involved. In such scenarios there is a well of suspicion that may need tackled, and this may be best done by via non-statutory services.

Positive practice considerations with non-resident fathers

- As with all fathers, non-resident fathers have a story to tell and there is a need to listen to this in the best interests of everyone.
- Becoming non-resident creates particular problems for parenting. Many participants attested to the difficulty of 'simulating' their child's home in a new abode. Fathers' unfamiliarity with a new role, a sense of artificiality, parenting beliefs or inhibitions appeared to contribute to unsatisfactory contact experiences with their children (Wilson *et al.*, 2004, p. 3).
- Non-resident fathers who moved out of the family home into

smaller accommodation or into friends' or relatives' homes were generally not able to have children to stay overnight. In some cases, this was a reasonably short-term issue, but for some parents it continued to remain a factor (Peacey and Hunt, 2009). When necessary, in the best interests of the child, practitioners need to advocate for such fathers to obtain accommodation that recognises their continuing parental responsibilities.

- Coupled with the above is that fact that many non-resident fathers have nowhere to bring the children to so as to have reasonable quality contact once they move out of the family home. The problem often is not just the amount of access *per se*, but where to have it, and in a place that does not cost a lot of money, be it the stereotypical McDonalds or some other commercial outlet. Again, this ought to be a straightforward matter for professionals to resolve, either by the provision of premises, having a list of fathers' projects that offer father–child opportunities, such as cookery or gardening, or other free and accessible fun activities, or by providing direct financial support for contact to take place, which might simply be the bus fares to and from a suitable location.
- Non-resident fathers can find themselves left out of information loops: for example, parent evenings and sports days; health and welfare checks. In child protection matters, social workers need to take special care to involve non-resident fathers who are regularly not included on lists for meetings, unless there is a significant reason for not doing so.
- There are particular issues for non-resident fathers with concerns about their children's welfare. Featherstone *et al.* remark that: 'Fathers noted the scepticism with which they were often treated by statutory agencies who appeared to assume automatically that the concerns were motivated by a desire to undermine their ex-partner. A number talked of being in a double bind. If they informed Social Services then contact might be made harder by the mother. They might then be less likely to be in a position to protect the children especially if Social Services failed to investigate their concerns or took no action' (Featherstone *et al.*, 2010, p. 11).
- Research consistently tells us that, in the absence of dedicated advice lines or knowledge of existing support, non-resident fathers

often turn to the law (Peacey and Hunt, 2009). Practitioners working with potential or actual non-resident fathers are advised to become familiar with existing father-facing services, such as local dads' workers, and more national services, such as the Fatherhood Institute.

Fathers in prison

Fathers in prison are obviously physically separated from their children and they may also be young fathers – estimates suggest that between 25% (Her Majesty's Inspectorate of Prisons, 1997) and 50% (Katz, 2002) of all young men in prison are fathers. More recent research suggests that in Polmont Young Offenders Institution in Scotland the figure is closer to one in three (Donnelly *et al.*, 2010). The proportion of all men in prison who have dependent children has been estimated at nearly 60% (Action for Prisoners' Families, 2010). In 2009, a Barnardo's study estimated that 160,000 children were affected annually by paternal incarceration (Glover, 2009). This number has undoubtedly increased.

Another way of putting the problem is posed by the Scottish charity Families Outside: 'Each year, an estimated 16,500 children in Scotland experience a parent's imprisonment; this means that a parent's imprisonment affects more children each year than divorce' (Loucks, 2012, p. 86). Without doubt the vast majority of these parents will be fathers.

Within the criminal justice system, fathering identities and the family responsibilities of fathers tend to remain invisible (Department of Economic and Social Affairs of the United Nations Secretariat, 2011). As for other categories of father, a familiar picture emerges of child welfare workers overlooking the importance of maintaining connections with imprisoned fathers, because they are thought of as either inaccessible to their children or uninvolved (Strug and Wilmore-Schaeffer, 2003).

Therefore, dedicated father-inclusive work needs to be systematically done with men in prison, both to assist them in maintaining contact with their children while inside, and to prepare them for (re-)entering an active fathering role on their release. The reasons are clear in that research tells us that recidivism levels are lower for men who re-enter fatherhood and relationships with their children and families (Meek, 2011). Children of prisoners are at risk from a host of factors. We know that nearly 60% of the sons of male prisoners will go on to offend and that early and maintained engagement with their fathers protects against this (Fathers Direct, 2004a). Studies have also shown that they are more likely than their peers to suffer from mental illness; they have a higher rate of truancy; and they are more likely to engage in antisocial behaviour.

However, if a worker decides to follow good practice and search for an incarcerated father they may not be told where to start. They may face some common challenges: no one may know where the father is located; people may be suspicious of his past criminal activity; and no one is quite sure where he fits into his child's life. Often, neither a child's parent nor carer with custody, nor the imprisoned parent, is prepared to address the needs of the children whose parents are in prison. Parents on the outside can be ambivalent about children's visits with their incarcerated parents and about what to tell children about their parent's reasons for being in jail. Some children do not know that their father is in jail, because they have been told that he is working away from home or in the Forces. If the child did not live with the parent and their time together was sporadic, the child may not be told anything about their father's absence. Some fathers do not want their children to visit them in prison and/or make no effort to contact their children. They do not believe the children's custodial parent will welcome such contact; they don't know where their children are; or they think such visits will be too emotionally painful. Some fathers in jail reason that they will be away only a short time and that there is no need for children to visit. Others mistakenly believe that there is little that they can do for their children from prison and that they can make it all up to them once they are released.

Positive practice with imprisoned fathers and their families

- Parenting programmes ought to be available to all fathers both expectant and existing. A number of studies confirm the positive attitudes of prisoners towards engaging in parenting education training while in custody:

'Once I heard about the Parenting Group that was going to start up, I was very interested. I did the course to get a stronger bond with my daughter. As part of the group we were to get a once in a lifetime chance to have a 2 hour visit where we could get to run around, do face-painting, read books, watch a video and so much more. Also apart from having the chance to spend two great hours with my daughter, there were certain things about the classroom work that I found interesting and thought I could pick up a few things from that' (father in Greenock prison, quoted in Clapton, 2003b, p. 15).

- Parenting programmes in prison have other benefits. 'Phoning home was an important topic. We discussed when phoning home and your children answer the phone not to ask for their mum straight away – something which I did. I learnt if you speak to them first asking about how was school and who they were playing with, it would make them feel important. I now ask to speak to my children all the time' (father in Greenock prison, quoted in Clapton, 2003b, p. 16).
- Greenock prison in Scotland was also one of the first establishments to encourage the use of storytelling by fathers to their children by means of video tapes. This is a highly effective means of maintaining the bond between father and child. It has been reported that the practice has been stopped in some prisons as it was abused by a minority. This is a regrettable and disproportionate reaction by prison authorities.
- Visits – the participants in Meek's study were clear that the best form of parenting support they could receive while in prison was 'help with maintaining contact with their children and families, with 75% of respondents emphasising the need for longer, more frequent or less disturbed visits with their children' (Meek, 2004, p. 245).
- A worry for the children of imprisoned fathers is whether anything about him will appear in the newspapers, providing fuel for taunts and bullying. The Ormiston Trust works with schools to ensure they have mechanisms in place to support children with a parent in prison. This ranges from using specially designed resources about the effects of prison, to making sure there is a designated person for affected children to talk to. The trust has also produced

a guide for teachers and other education professionals about working with the children of prisoners (available at URL: www.ormiston.org/our-services/families-affected-by-imprisonment; accessed 17 December 2012).

- Fathers in the Learning Together Project at HMP Parc in Wales follow the school curriculum along with their children, then help with their homework when the children come into the prison (Loucks, 2012).
- Sentencing – while women's maternal status is regularly considered when reports are prepared, men's paternal connections rarely are (Department of Economic and Social Affairs of the United Nations Secretariat, 2011). Background reports ought routinely to discuss fathers' bonds with their children and their responsibilities.

Stepfathers

It is acknowledged that there are a number of other categories of fathers with whom social work will be involved. Stepfathers, for example, are at particular risk of being ignored by social workers who see themselves as working with women and children. A growing body of research demonstrates the value of stepfathers to mothers and stepchildren (Marsiglio and Hinojosa, 2010) and highlights the importance of differentiating among the diverse types of social fathers in children's lives. Any work with men as stepfathers or father-figures in families requires an assessment of just how involved the man is in the family's life. To establish whether the man is a casual acquaintance of the mother's, a transient partner or a man committed to being, or trying to live a life as, a father to the children can be a complex endeavour. The interplay of some men's avoidance of family responsibilities, coupled with social workers giving up on what can be perceived as disinterested or ambivalent men, can lead to them being ignored or bypassed when in fact these 'unofficial' fathers may be a huge resource. In Ferguson and Hogan's study:

> Some stepfathers were recognised to be a huge resource for the family to an extent where children were either not taken into care or were returned to mothers and their new partners because of the stability and care the latter now offered the

> family (Ferguson and Hogan, 2004, pp. 15–16).

Workers must also be aware that the research indicates that 'an intrinsically protective mechanism is not "switched" on with non-biological fathers who come later into the family' (Pritchard *et al.*, 2012). However, the same writers go on to note that: 'Conversely, a non-violent, non-abusing stepfather joining a family can be very positive for the child and help to raise the family out of poverty' (ibid., p. 24).

Lone fathers

There are two million lone-parent families, and according to Gingerbread (2012) around 8% of single parents (186,000) are fathers. Recent research on the experiences, needs and perspectives of lone fathers is thin on the ground. However, what is known is that there are many pathways to becoming a lone father, including resolution of a custody issue, divorce, temporary or permanent absence, or death of partner. What is also known is that lone fathers may need additional considerations as they may find it difficult to develop supportive social networks and may feel stigmatised as a result of being a lone, male carer. Despite the lack of research there are many self-help websites. The following is taken from an Edinburgh group for lone fathers and is typical of the reasons for their establishment:

> The majority of the father's concerns were their own socioeconomic position, alcohol and drug misuse, bullying, racism, violence, low levels of self-esteem and self confidence. Additional issues were the lack of family support as very few of the fathers had an extended family to rely on. There was no one to guide them or influence them with their parenting skills. Many felt anger or frustration as a result of feeling unacknowledged. None of the fathers was aware of any other resource, apart from the project, which addressed the issues related to being a lone/contact father (www.meninchildcare.co.uk/Develop.htm; accessed January 2013).

Some less known of categories of fathers

There are a number of other categories of father that could either be developed from the ones that have been given precedence in this chapter or present their own set of special needs and challenges (and strengths): for example, gay fathers and minority ethnic fathers. The literature relating to the particular position of such groups and child and family welfare tends to be much less in evidence; however, the website of the Fatherhood Institute is a good place to begin a search. In special relation to black fathers, the already mentioned research findings in the Fathers Matter initiative of the FRG merit reading (Ashley *et al.*, 2006).

****

This chapter has focused on working with fathers, and there will be times in this process when workers will need to advocate for fathers. Practice that avoids a singular 'fathers' rights' approach has shown to be the most positive in achieving the best outcomes for fathers and their children and families. However, there are times when workers will be required to know the legal position, often in something as basic as the importance of a father having his name on the child's birth certificate. At other times (e.g. when care proceedings, such as adoption, are taking place), skilled advocacy may be required.

With some groups of under-informed fathers, advocacy may be essential. This chapter has already drawn attention to young fathers whose relative lack of knowledge of the 'system' may disadvantage them. However, other categories of fathers may also benefit from representation and advocacy: for example, fathers with learning disabilities; fathers who cannot read or write; fathers in prison; and fathers with English as a second language.

It is acknowledged that many of the fathers discussed above might also fall into the 'risky' category, but this chapter has been dedicated to laying out the principle and practice of positive working with all fathers. The next chapter will outline practice with a particular cross-cutting category of fathers with whom children and families workers are frequently engaged – those who are or may be a risk to children and their partners and/or those who may express violence and aggression in their dealings with workers.

Key research and resources

Think Family Toolkit: Improving Support for Families at Risk: Strategic Overview. Initiative by DCSF. Available at URL: www.education.gov.uk/publications/eOrderingDownload/Think-Family.pdf (accessed 17 December 2012)

'Good helping relationships in child welfare' by C. de Boer and N. Cody, *Child and Family Social Work*, Vol. 12, No. 1 (2007), pp. 32–42

The Fatherhood Institute has published a highly valuable series of research briefings on the various categories of fathers discussed in this chapter. Available at URL: www.fatherhoodinstitute.org (accessed 17 December 2012)

SPECIFIC PARENTING PROGRAMMES

There is no one fatherhood programme model. Some are informal support groups started locally (these are discussed in the chapter for fathers' workers); some address the special issues that affect fathers parenting children with special needs; others are structured to work with fathers holistically to address stressors or behaviours that can affect their abilities to support their children emotionally and financially (such as unemployment, lone-parenting or non-custodial); and still others work with incarcerated fathers or those involved in family violence. Some are small, local activities, while others collaborate with larger social service agencies. Programmes that promote an authoritative style of parenting and/or support the co-parenting alliance are particularly likely to improve outcomes for fathers and their children. Examples of such programmes include the Incredible Years, Triple P, the Supporting Father Involvement Project and the Marriage and Parenting in Stepfamilies Intervention. All have undergone at least one randomised controlled trial and have demonstrated improvements in both fathers' and children's behaviour (Asmussen and Weizel, 2010).

www.incredibleyears.com (accessed 17 December 2012)

www.triplep.net (accessed 17 December 2012)

www.supportingfatherinvolvement.org (accessed 17 December 2012)

www.oslc.org/projects/popups-projects/marriage-parent-stepf.html (accessed 17 December 2012)

CHAPTER 5

Assessing and Working with Risk with Fathers

> 'To move toward true inclusiveness in both protecting and supporting children, practitioners need to proactively assess and engage with all significant men in a child's life, understanding that some may pose risks, some may be assets and some may incorporate aspects of both' (Strega *et al.*, 2008, p. 713).
>
> 'Mr B's aggressive attitude has resulted in staff declining to work with him' (a typical case note).

The feelings of many fathers such as Mr B may include anger, suspicion, powerlessness and a number of other debilitating emotions that, in men, can be displayed as aggression, combativeness or threatening behaviour towards practitioners. When violence is present towards children and partners, then men responsible for this may also resort to a combination of deviousness and defensiveness. The causes for such men's behaviour will remain a permanent debating matter (see below, 'Why can fathers be cruel?'). However, what is emerging from the research is that a father who is a risk in a family cannot be ignored (or 'staff decline to work' with a father because of his perceived aggressiveness), because, even should he part company with his children and partner or move out of the family, then: firstly, his children and he may continue to be in contact with one another; secondly, he may return or be invited back; and, thirdly, if not, he may establish a home with another woman and children, or go on to have additional children. It is for these reasons that fathers who have been a risk to their children and partners should not be ignored or sighs of relief breathed when they move out.

WHY CAN FATHERS BE CRUEL?

There are certain characteristics of fathers that can make them more likely to mistreat a child. Poverty, underemployment or unemployment can increase a father's stress level, which may make him more likely to physically mistreat his children. Underemployment and unemployment also undermine a father's feelings of self-worth, which may make him more likely to lash out at his children. Substance abuse also is strongly associated with higher rates of abuse and neglect among fathers and mothers. One study found that 66% of children raised in alcoholic homes were physically maltreated or witnessed domestic violence and that more than 25% of these children were sexually abused (Buchanan, 1996). Additionally, fathers who were abused or who witnessed domestic violence between their parents are more likely to hurt their own children. Among other things, substance abuse lowers the inhibitions that fathers might otherwise have in connection with abusing their children by diminishing self-control. Fathers with a low sense of self-worth are also more likely to hurt their children. Those experiencing psychological distress or low self-esteem may seek diversion from their problems or may abuse their children as a way to dominate and thus to derive a perverse sense of personal power. Fathers also may maltreat their children as a way of exacting revenge on a spouse or partner by whom they feel humiliated (adapted from Rosenberg and Wilcox, 2006)

Social workers must engage with the many fathers who are a *resource*, yet display some of the emotions referred to above. Anger, suspicion and combativeness are not uncommon in both fathers and mothers involved in child protection, and social workers regularly negotiate these in the best interests of children. However, this chapter focuses on fathers who display such emotions *and* have been harmful towards their children and partners, or may be a risk to them.

How can the research help?

As already noted, much social work thinking, writing and practice relating to fathers in child protection can be organised into three categories: the absent father; the father as unimportant; and the dangerous father. It is the last category that is dominant in the child protection practice discourse. Lee *et al.* point out that: 'Most existing research on fathers and child protection emphasises risk rather than protective factors' (Lee *et al.*, 2009, p. 227). Yet, firstly, a failure to consider fathers (and paternal networks) as a resource in child protection is a fundamental flaw in any child-centred assessment of risk and protective factors. In 60% of the child protection case conferences in Farmer and Owen's study (1998), the issue of whether the mother could protect the child was considered, whereas the possibility of the father as protector of the child was examined in just 19% of cases. If 'bringing in' the non-abusive father is uncontested, what of the father who has hurt his child or partner? Practitioners cannot proceed as if he does not or ought not to exist. Peled points out that:

> Many children of abusive men care deeply for their fathers and wish they could have a gratifying relationship with them. Further, if we believe that parents are responsible for the well-being of their children, and that both parents are to share this responsibility, we can no longer ignore the role of abusive men as fathers (Peled, 2000, p. 29).

What have we learnt from the little research on working with maltreating fathers? Rivett (2010) provides an important starting point. Rather than the binary approach of either risk or resource, regarding men who are a risk as *both a risk and a resource* offers a way forward. Rivett goes on to develop this *both/and* perspective. He argues that such men are often both violent and also fathers/stepfathers. They are often both abusive and keen to be better fathers/partners; they can be both dangerous and open to change. Rivett concludes, citing Perel and Peled (2008), that any approach to violent male carers should see them 'as simultaneously harmful and vulnerable' (Rivett, 2010, p. 478) and that such approaches should avoid 'one-dimensional' descriptions' (ibid., p. 205).

This more nuanced approach to the lived reality of fathers and their families also chimes with one of the conclusions of Brandon *et al.* in their analysis of serious case reviews, when they observe that professionals held:

rigid or fixed thinking about men as 'all good' or 'all bad' and it therefore being possible, for example, 'to discount a bad dad's concern about the welfare of the children in his ex-wife's care' (Brandon *et al.*, 2009, p. 52).

Maxwell *et al.* (2012b) observe that little is known about which approaches to engaging men who have been violent are the most effective, but, in practical terms, they go on to suggest an approach that draws on the theory and skills of motivational interviewing could be promising. Motivational interviewing is a directive style of therapeutic engagement, which aims to enhance motivation to change through the resolution of ambivalence (Miller and Rollnick, 2002) and has been shown to be effective with reluctant service users (e.g. people who substance-abuse). Such a combination of direct approach and trust-building coupled with helping men understand the negative effects of their behaviour on their children seems a worthy way forward. This approach of fathers as both a risk and a resource is then a practical alternative to any excluding 'hands-off' tendency that works to ignore the complexities involved in cases where fathers have been violent; among other things, this tendency places a greater burden on mothers (Scott and Crooks, 2004).

Following the framework used in the last chapter, the next section is divided into the components of positive practice. As in work with all fathers, work with fathers' anger or aggression – or with fathers who are or may be a risk to children and partners – requires most of the same attributes: for example, a self-knowledge and a positive attitude towards the potential of good fathering; a sound knowledge base for advocacy; and the ability for straight-talking and to listen and encourage men to tell their stories. However, there are some specific attributes to be stressed in this chapter.

Attitudes

Simply put, it is impossible to be without biases and preconceptions about fathers. For any professional working with men, especially caseworkers in the very difficult and emotionally charged realm of child protective services, it is important to recognise and understand one's own biases and preconceptions (Rosenberg and Wilcox, 2006, p. 25).

The presence of violence alleged, assumed or established cannot be avoided; however, Rivett argues that approaches that work with violent male carers should go:

> *beyond the violent label*. These men will continue to be carers for their children and their relationship with those children will outlast most of the interventions provided therefore their role as carers must also be addressed (Rivett, 2010, pp. 198–9; emphasis in original).

So how does positive practice proceed in such circumstances? The next discussion breaks down the elements of intervention into assessment, engagement, positive work and strategies for supporting positive practice.

Assessment

The following draws on the work of Rosenberg and Wilcox (2006). Whether in the home or not, when there has been a suggestion of child maltreatment, the worker should:

- understand what type of relationship the father has with his child and the family;
- learn about how the father of the child fits into the current family dynamics;
- understand what role the father plays either in contributing to the circumstances that led to maltreatment or in helping to protect the child from further maltreatment.

An assessment or investigation cannot be considered complete until these issues are addressed and understood to the fullest extent possible.

The first decision point in the assessment process is substantiating that maltreatment actually occurred. The second decision point is assessing risk. Risk assessment involves evaluating the child and family's situation to identify and weigh the risk factors, family strengths and resources, and agency and community services. Assessing risk involves gathering information in four key domains: the maltreatment itself; the child; caregivers; and family functioning.

Fathers clearly need to be interviewed as part of the assessment or investigation. This is recommended whether the father is living with the child or not. The reasons why it is important to interview fathers who live outside the home include the following:

- The father is significant to the child, whether the father is actively involved in the child's life or not.
- The non-residential father has an important impact on the dynamics of the family.
- If placement outside of the home should be necessary, the biological father may prove to be a suitable placement.
- The non-residential father may play a role in ameliorating the circumstances that led to the harm.

During an assessment, workers should be aware of some unique issues relevant to fathers that may prove useful in understanding the father's role in the family. For fathers who live in the home, workers should address the following topics:

- What role does the father view himself playing in the family?
- How does the father view the maltreatment that occurred? Does he see it as a failure on his part? Does he experience the fact that his child was maltreated as an affront as to how he views himself as a man and a father?
- Is there anything he personally believes he could have done differently to prevent the maltreatment?
- What role models as a father has he himself had? How does the father believe these role models would or should have handled the situation that led to the maltreatment?
- If the father was the perpetrator, it will be important to explore his views of discipline and punishment and how he came to learn what is appropriate discipline. It will also be important to explore the role of aggression and anger in the father's life to help determine the risk the father may present in the future. Is he, for example, open to learning new ways of discipline?
- What is the relationship between the father and the mother of the child(ren), and how does he interact with her?
- Are there other men involved with the family, how does the father view these men, and what is the type and quality of their relationship?

For fathers who live outside the child's home, topics to explore include:

- What is the current living arrangement of the father *vis-à-vis* the home in which his child lives?
- Is there another man living in the home with the child? How does the child's father view this man and his relationship with his child and the mother of his child?
- How often does the father see his child? If and when he does see the child, what is the nature of the interaction?

Assuming that a father is or has been violent, then what next?

Engagement with violence

Interrogating violence

Malm *et al.* argue that:

> Unless safety concerns are effectively addressed, both those related to worker safety as well as those related to the safety of the child and mother, efforts to involve fathers are likely to stall. Safety concerns need to be acknowledged and assessed at a case level and through training (Malm *et al.*, 2006, p. 165).

They go on to note the fact that: 'nearly half of the fathers were never contacted by the agency suggests that little assessment of the actual risk presented is occurring' (Malm *et al.*, 2006). This suggests that workers need to uncouple fear of men's violence from the reasonable expectation of its existence. Scourfield's (2001) findings that the predominant construction of men as a threat continues to resonate, and many practitioners continue to adopt an approach that is wary or at least hesitant of fathers. However, Featherstone notes that:

> In terms of men who are physically violent the notion of a universal threat that appears to feed social work discourses also needs deconstructing. For example, although it is assumed that men who are violent to women clients will be violent to women workers, research indicates that most assaults on social workers are from women clients and also that male social workers are more likely to be targets than women (Featherstone, 2003, pp. 250–1).

So in interrogating either allegations of violence (in case notes or otherwise) it is important that workers unpack whether what has been depicted as aggressive behaviour could in fact be frustration, borne from inarticulacy, helplessness or inability to comprehend child protection systems – some things common to most parents who experience these.

Nonetheless, men do cause harm to their children and partners. These men ought not to be 'let off the parenting hook' (Peled, 2000). If they are to be reached in the interests of their children, and future children and partners, workers must find ways to engage, yet we know little of their point of view, their version of the precipitating triggers and their feelings at the time. It is as if their actions have placed them forever beyond the pale (Guille, 2004). Ferguson and Hogan's study of fathers and their families in Ireland is one of the few that seeks to get inside the heads of men who they describe as vulnerable fathers:

> Our findings show, categorically, that the front that vulnerable fathers present to the outside world (including social workers) constantly belies the active, nurturing side of themselves that they may express in private. Similar things can be said about men who have been separated from their children through the legal/court system and how their (riotous) anger and politicised discourse in relation to father's rights can also distract professional attention from the fact that these fathers are hurting, and what they and their children need (Ferguson and Hogan, 2004, p. 160).

In the best interests of children, partners and fathers themselves, workers need to think and act beyond any experience or reputation of a man as dangerous. This is not to say that danger should be ignored, rather the challenge is:

> take seriously any evidence of destructive, violent behaviour while understanding the expression of anger as being an exterior expression of some deeper, interior malaise such as pain, sadness, loneliness or other such emotion that men have been socially conditioned to repress (Ferguson and Hogan, 2004, p. 175).

Positive practice

Ferguson and Hogan go on to advance a useful approach to engaging positively with fathers who have been violent:

> The notion of vulnerability we adopted included a wide range of experiences, from men who were vulnerable to being violent to their children and/or partners or were known to have already been, to those who were experiencing a range of problems, including 'marital' breakdown, relationship and communication problems with their children, poverty and the impact of extreme social exclusion, surviving child sexual abuse, addictions, and domestic violence (Ferguson and Hogan, 2004, p. 7).

Engagement with maltreating fathers on the basis that they are vulnerable helps balance perceptions that they are beyond rehabilitation and has much merit. It is acknowledged that some such fathers may need to be compelled to meet with workers; however, whether by agreement or not, once a worker and a father have met, what is possible? Scott and Crooks argue that:

> intervening with abusive fathers is a worthwhile goal. However, intervention must go beyond providing skills or support. Instead, treatment must challenge deeply held beliefs and foster a new child-centered perspective. Although a formidable challenge, the potential benefits in preventing future abuse and in redressing damage already done justifies the effort. By providing fathers with the opportunity to take responsibility for their past abuse and to engage with their children in a more empathetic and nurturing way, we have an opportunity to teach new lessons about being men and perhaps to open a window to break the cycle of violence (Scott and Crooks, 2004, p. 108).

Some key starting points for positive engagement with these fathers will include:

- not excusing but recasting the behaviours of these fathers as derived from material pressures or historic circumstances;
- an appreciation that these men have little or no idea of the adverse effect that their behaviour has on their children;

- building in extrinsic motivational factors, such as the return (or loss) of their children;
- being alert to the importance to the men of their maintaining a positive image of themselves (Stanley *et al.*, 2012).

Once engagement has happened, some key principles for workers with men who are or have been violent are:

- Social workers should not put themselves at risk or endanger the safety of mothers and children (Daniel and Taylor, 2001).
- Intervention should assume that there may be little initial motivation to change: 'Maltreating fathers typically do not seek intervention voluntarily, nor are they intrinsically motivated to change their parenting style' (Scott and Crooks, 2004, p. 101).
- Men who maltreat need to understand that the relationship they have with their children is not independent of the relationship they have with the children's mother. Scott and Crooks argue: 'that being a good father requires that they avoid or end abuse against their children's mother and that they develop a relationship with her that is respectful' (Scott and Crooks, 2004, p. 104).

Setting key goals is also necessary.

Goals

Workers with fathers who have hurt or neglected their children need to help these fathers to:

- address any factors that may have led up to their perpetration of maltreatment;
- be honest about the fact that they have a problem and need to take active steps to prevent future acts of maltreatment. The crucial first step these parents must take is to acknowledge what they have done;
- acknowledge that their actions were wrong and harmful. They should reflect specifically on the harm they have done to their child, which is a crucial step in helping them to desist from further harm;

- apologise to their children, either in person or in writing, both to acknowledge their own culpability and to help their children recover from the harm. Few would fail to support reparative behaviour by mothers, and there is no reason to believe that reparation by fathers would be entirely without value to most children. Fathers who do cease their maltreatment and take accountability for past hurt can send a powerful message to their children, breaking a potential cycle of multigenerational child abuse;
- identify the psychological and situational stressors and stimuli (e.g. loneliness, drug or alcohol use, being alone with their child in the evening) that led to physical or sexual abuse and avoid these at all costs;
- learn appropriate disciplinary principles and techniques. Physical maltreatment is often linked to unrealistic expectations or rigid attitudes. By learning about the developmental stages of children (e.g. in parenting sessions/briefings – don't call these classes), fathers can develop appropriate rules, expectations and behaviour.

Additionally, drawing on the observations made in the previous chapters, this work, while never losing sight of the seriousness of maltreatment, may need to be undertaken in less official surroundings and workers ought to have a flexibility that allows for the use of the more usual and local settings in which men voice a need for help (often in the form of asking for advice), fathers' groups, GP surgeries or during health visitors' visits.

Reconciliation between a father and his child – especially in cases of sexual abuse or multiple incidents of physical harm – will necessarily be difficult. Indeed, involved family members, child protection workers and the courts will often legitimately decide that a father can no longer live with his children as a consequence of his physical or sexual abuse. Nevertheless, research on restorative justice suggests that some contact, even if it is brief, between the father and his child may be helpful to all concerned parties if the father takes responsibility for his actions and expresses contrition (Braithwaite, 2002). Thus, professionals and family members seeking to address a father's maltreatment of his child may wish to consider some effort at reconciliation, provided that both the father and the child (along with the mother or guardian) consent to such an effort.

Risk and multiple fathers

A situation that can be extremely challenging occurs when there are multiple fathers involved in the family. In some families, children are living in the same household, yet have different fathers. There may be different arrangements: the mother is living with children by herself, while the fathers of the children may or may not be involved; the mother may be living with the father of one or more of her children, while the father(s) of her other children may or may not be involved; and the mother may be living with a man who is not the father of any of her children, and the father(s) of her children may or may not be involved (Goff, 2012). Obviously, any one of these scenarios presents the potential for tension and confusion over roles. Concerns over who is responsible for the safety of the children, who plays the role of the psychological father – the man who acts, in the eyes of the child, as 'dad' – and how other adults are portraying the father to his children will come into play. Financial issues are often a source of tension. Issues of trust between and among the adults are almost sure to arise. As one would expect, it is common for one father to be angry at another over who is responsible for a child being maltreated.

When working with a family with multiple fathers involved, it is important for workers to understand the role each man plays in the family dynamic. It is also essential to learn how each father views the maltreatment, what led up to it, and who, in his mind, is responsible for the maltreatment occurring. All men living in the household should be part of the process, including family meetings. Whether and when to involve other fathers of children in the household needs to be determined on a case-by-case basis and, like any challenging issue facing a worker, supervision can be a valuable tool. The goal of the entire process, of course, is to achieve safety for the child. One or all of the fathers who are connected to the family can prove to be a valuable ally in accomplishing this goal.

Risk and boyfriends/surrogate fathers

While he is not the father, a boyfriend may fill the role of father to the child. He may contribute financially to rearing the child. He may be the father of other children in the house, but not of the child who was maltreated. If the father of the child who was maltreated is involved in any way, the father assuredly will have strong feelings about the boyfriend. Much has been written about boyfriends in the house and their role in child maltreatment. Because these men typically do not have the same history of care and nurturing with the child, the same emotional and normative commitment to the child's welfare, and the same institutionalised role as a father-figure as do biological fathers in intact families, boyfriends pose a higher risk to children if they spend time alone with them. Mothers' boyfriends, for example, are much more likely to be involved in physical or sexual abuse of children than a biological father. In one study of physical maltreatment, boyfriends accounted for 64% of non-parental abuse, even though boyfriends performed only 2% of non-parental care (Finkelhor *et al.*, 1997). Another study found that the odds of child maltreatment were 2.5 times higher in households with a boyfriend living in the home, compared to households with a biological father (Radhakrishna *et al.*, 2001). The authors of the latter study conclude that child protection workers should 'focus more of their attention on the high-risk relationship between a surrogate father and the children' (Radhakrishna *et al.*, 2001, pp. 34–5).

Supervising positive practice

Given the nature of child protection work, it is likely that the practitioner will be involved with the family at a time of tension and/or conflict, which may confirm established gender stereotypes. Indeed, gender stereotyping is a feature in deciding which practitioner would undertake the assessment, with some explicit expectations that, when fathers were deemed aggressive or angry with workers, then male colleagues would be the nominated worker or there would be a co-working arrangement. Supervisors need to be alert to such pressures. Reid and Murphy acknowledge that: 'Practitioners also find it difficult to work inclusively with both parents when one is accusing the other of harming the child' (Reid and Murphy, 2009, p.

17), and in such cases supervisors will need to consider two workers, not necessarily a male for the father and a female for the mother, with the proviso of caution as to the potential for worker conflict.

Supervisors also need to ask themselves: 'Is this work suitable for newly qualified practitioners?' Huebner *et al.* observe that 'engaging fathers in child protective services is an emotional issue' (2008, p. 99), and supervisors will need to bear in mind the demanding nature of the work in which varying sets of emotions (including their own) may result in workers feeling like emotional blotting paper.

Likewise, practice teachers need to think about the appropriateness of a student undertaking the kind of practice indicated above. However, as in many cases, practice wisdom can be mixed with a father-excluding 'canteen culture' of much of statutory child protection. Franck (2001) suggests that approaches to engaging fathers do not appear to alter appreciably with greater experience. The relative clean sheet that new workers and students bring to a case can be refreshing and productive. However, when engaged in work where there is a likelihood of interpersonal conflict and emotions run high (remembering that in the case of men these may be expressed in what can be perceived as angry and threatening manners), every practitioner needs access to a supervisor. Given that some of this work may be 'out of hours', so as to fit around a father's work and leisure patterns, this may also mean that, equally, supervisory support ought to be available then.

HOW DO YOU REMEMBER YOUR FATHER?

Previous chapters have noted that a 'way in' to fathers' thoughts, feelings and ultimately actions may be engaging him in discussion about his experiences of being fathered, or not.

One writer identifies a type of depression unique to men, which he calls 'male depression', the underlying cause of which is early childhood abandonment by fathers (Real, 1997). Depression in men often goes undiagnosed because the great majority do not exhibit classical symptoms of major depression, such as observable apathy and sadness. Depressed men often don't look depressed but instead wear a variety of disguises. Real refers to 'the many masks of male depression', which may linger for years and ultimately impact parenting. One of these masks is characterised by the continuum of anger, rage and violence. Male socialisation rarely gives men permission to express vulnerable emotions, such as sadness and hurt, which would be normal and expected following father abandonment. Instead, men are taught to hide their vulnerability.

Repressed emotions then often emerge in the form of anger, making it difficult for others to suspect that the angry father may actually be depressed. Rage is the end result of anger that has built up over extended periods of time, and violent behaviour may be the offshoot of repressed rage. Children and partners may be the targets of a father's anger, rage and/or violence. Anger does not eliminate the physical drain of depression. In truth, a depressed father, lacking the energy to contribute to household matters, pushes others to take over his responsibilities. Secretly, a father may have feelings of failure as a man, spouse, partner and parent. The sense of failure can exacerbate depression and increase isolation, including isolation from his kids. Many men respond to feelings of depression and failure by engaging in numbing behaviours, which may include heavy substance use or substituting substance use with process addictions, such as compulsive gambling, overeating, cyberspace addiction and promiscuity. These behaviours may move him even further away from his children (adapted from Sanders, 2009).

****

This chapter has been written in the knowledge of other models for working with men who have been violent or, as named in some of this literature, are 'batterers', 'perpetrators' 'abusers' etc. The 'Duluth' model (named after the place of its origin in the USA) is one such intervention, which is psycho-educational in nature and confronts and shames men who have been violent (Morran, 2011). The Duluth model has been in existence since the 1970s, yet the evidence base for change remains weak (Stover *et al.*, 2009) with one meta-analysis of outcomes concluding that 'the mean effect for victim reported outcomes was zero' (Feder and Wilson, 2005, p. 239). Morran argues that the voices of men who have been violent are difficult to listen to, but where these are:

> simply drowned out, and the man presented with a template which 'brands' or labels him simply as a 'perpetrator', then his resistance to engagement is heightened from the outset (Morran, 2011, p. 29).

The perspective offered here – and indeed throughout this book – is one based on a strengths-based ethos, not a deficit-driven ideology.

Finally, on the question of positive practice with fathers who are or have been violent, as already noted, the development of a strengths-based ethos at practice level will be immensely boosted if such an approach can be mirrored at local and central government levels. With the holistic perspective of the Scottish Government's (2012) *Getting It Right For Every Child* initiative and its national parenting strategy having taken pains to solicit the views of fathers in its consultative process, there is a great opportunity for Scottish policymakers to get this right. However, other policy planks such as *The Early Years Framework* (Scottish Government, 2009) and the *National Guidance for Child Protection in Scotland* (Scottish Government, 2010) have some way to go in including fathers both in their texts and images.

The next chapter discusses how the strengths-based ethos can be translated within agencies and taken into training and teaching.

Key research and resources

A US survey of fathers' participation in Family Group Conferences (FGC) showed that in 62% of cases fathers attended FGCs (Thoennes, 2003). This contrasts with research by Thoburn *et al.* (1995), which found fathers to be present at only 16% of child protection case conferences.

Strengthening Families Through Fathers: Developing Policy and Practice in Relation to Vulnerable Fathers and Their Families, H. Ferguson and F. Hogan (2004). Available at URL: http://repository.wit.ie/676/1/foreword.pdf (accessed 17 December 2012)

The Importance of Fathers in the Healthy Development of Children, J. Rosenberg and W. Wilcox (2006), especially Chapter 3. Available at URL: www.childwelfare.gov/pubs/usermanuals/fatherhood/fatherhood.pdf (accessed 17 December 2012)

Caring Dads is an intervention programme designed explicitly for fathers that have physically abused, emotionally abused or neglected their children, or exposed their children to domestic violence or who are deemed to be at high risk for these behaviours. A UK probation-based programme has been running since 2005. Details available at URL: www.london-probation.org.uk/what_we_do/caring_dads.aspx (accessed 17 December 2012)

See also the successful Mellow Dads programme in West Lothian. Details available at URL: http://makinggenderequalityreal.org.uk/mellow-dadsthe-dads-club-west-lothian-sure-start (accessed 17 December 2012)

DAVE'S STORY

In a Scottish survey of fathers' involvement in FGCs, one father is quoted:

> Dave gave a particularly vivid description of his feelings of frustration and helplessness: 'At social work meetings, you feel that every move is being watched. It's a waste of time speaking because nobody listens. In a meeting room with suits and ties, you feel undermined, people looking over their glasses at you. You do feel judged.' He went on to contrast this with the FGC: 'At the FGC we had more freedom to speak, we didn't feel the same stress.'

One FGC could do more than twenty meetings in a clinical environment (Ross, 2006, p. 18).

CHARLOTTE'S STORY

'I was given paper, stamps and envelopes to write out the invitations (*to the family group conference*) myself. This was good because my dad wouldn't have liked an official-looking letter as he hated social services. We got to choose the venue ourselves, which was great too because my dad wouldn't be seen going into a social service building. He still made loads of excuses why he couldn't come though, so we worked it around him so he had to come! It was held at 8.30 on a Wednesday evening in a local hotel ... We argued, we cried, we laughed and we cried again. I think we must have been in there two hours before we asked everyone to come back in, but we had achieved so much. In that room that night I learnt so much about each person in there, and I know they would say the same. I learnt that, even though he doesn't always show it, my dad really loves me, because he was there' (quoted in Fathers Direct, 2004b).

See www.frg.org.uk/the-family-group-conference-process (accessed 17 December 2012) for more on FGCs.

CHAPTER 6

Positive Agency and Teaching Practice with Fathers

Positive practice with fathers is in its infancy, and, as noted by Page *et al.* (2008), there is a tendency for this to be somewhat of a 'one-man' band in that, in an agency or team or in a faculty, father-focused discussion will normally be instigated by an individual taking an interest in the issue. There will be always be opposition but it is rare that there will be a collective impetus for an entire team or workplace to commit to the kind of principles, attitudes and practices outlined in the previous chapters. This is not a million miles away from the earlier challenges of developing anti-racist and anti-discriminatory practice. This has led to some campaigners, such as the Fatherhood Institute, calling for mainstreaming father-inclusive policies and, for example, guidance and training materials to be 'father-proofed' (Clapton, 2012). This chapter discusses strategies for getting fathers on the agenda in your workplace and provides some suggestions for training and teaching about fathers.

Encouraging positive father practice in the field

At a team level

Engaging and including fathers is not as simple as expecting service providers to do their jobs differently. Service providers' service orientations and the service possibilities open to them are shaped substantially by the system that employs them. So where to start? Firstly, knowing more about fathers' lives and their experiences with child welfare will enable some frontline service providers to be more productive in their approaches to fathers and families. Secondly, there is likely to be a fathers' worker in the neighbourhood who can be invited to the team or used as a resource. (The next chapter looks at the activities of fathers' workers and the expansion of groups offering support for fathers.)

If there is not a worker in the neighbourhood, then there are a number of websites and publications available online that can be used as stimulants to a team discussion. Research in one UK local authority found:

> widespread recognition, in theory, of the importance of working with fathers as part of a holistic approach to supporting individual children and families, and several examples of workers actively seeking out men and welcoming their contribution. Discussions demonstrated that many recognised that the socialisation of boys and young men, from all cultural backgrounds, depended critically on improving the level and quality of their contact with their fathers and on their fathers experiencing services as accessible, welcoming and supportive. There were examples of positive professional discourses and of teams demonstrating strong commitment to reflective practice, and to understanding diversity (Gilligan *et al.*, 2012, p. 514).

However, the research also found that very few teams could identify specific examples of concrete actions and practices that reflected the widespread recognition that fathers needed to be more included in child protection activity. For a continuing while though, until organisational change is effected, it is likely that there will be one 'go to' guy for advice regarding fathers.

Training has been found to impact some casework practices. In a US study, differences were found between cases with workers who had received training on identifying, locating and engaging non-resident fathers and cases in which the worker had not been trained. Workers were more likely to seek assistance with locating the father from other workers, the mother's relatives and father's relatives in cases in which the worker reported having received training (Malm *et al.*, 2006, p. 125).

There have been other calls for training for practitioners to work more confidently and successfully with adult males: 'so that they become more capable of both supporting positive male involvement and protecting children from negative male influences' (Bellamy, 2009, p. 260). On the other hand, exercises that stop at just consciousness-raising have their limitations (as was the case in tackling racism in the 1970s and 1980s in the UK), with any lessons learnt dissipated in the absence of both an ongoing commitment to change at organisational and structural level and the opportunity to deploy practical practice suggestions for change.

Specific pointers for positive practice at a team or workplace level include the following:

- Work towards fathers being seen as the team's responsibility, as part of 'core business' (e.g. provide regular briefings about latest developments).
- Workers, male or female: 'who develop the capacity to sit with vulnerable men and call forth their stories set up a positive developmental dynamic within organisations as more positive images of men and stories about effective engagement become part of the culture' (Ferguson and Hogan, 2004, p. 17).
- Staff and managers should have opportunities to: explore their attitudes/beliefs about dads in general and local dads in particular; explore and challenge assumptions; identify gaps in knowledge; and acknowledge disagreement.
- Help staff see that non-engagement by services with fathers does not reduce risks.
- Review forms. Records should have a space for 'mother' and 'father', referrals should be questioned that do not refer to a birth father or key father-figures, and bear in mind that not all these men are referred to as fathers or biological fathers (Maxwell *et al.*, 2012a).
- 'Limit your use of the "P" word! P is for parent and most fathers don't feel included when it is used' (Fathers Direct, 2007).
- Fathers grow in the presence of caring staff who model the kind of relationship they can have with their children and who demonstrate a belief in their strength and potential. If staff demonstrate, however unconsciously, negative

stereotypes toward a man, they will lose any chance of connecting with him and, even worse, they may undermine his self-esteem and set in motion a self-fulfilling prophecy that leads to actual negative behaviour (Bartlett and Vann, 2004).

- To see only the positives in fathers can put workers or families at risk, will not provide effective support to the men and will alienate colleagues. Finding ways of allowing staff to identify and name negative behaviour without stopping there are essential to successful interventions (Bartlett and Vann, 2004).

Ultimately, child welfare teams, agencies and workplaces that 'see' fathers and provide policy and practice guidance about engaging with fathers will, in the long term, reduce the risk of harm to children and mothers (Walmsley, 2009). This applies at a wider level too.

On an organisational or departmental level

Ferguson and Hogan recommend an agency-wide strategy to ensure that staff are trained in the skills of 'father-advocacy' and that specialist posts of 'father-advocates' are created, and call for staff support and care in a move that would benefit more than fathers:

> Not only routine agency supervision but systematic forms of therapeutic support need to be provided for professionals by agencies. Such systematic self-reflection needs to be part of ongoing professional practice and development. Again, the biggest challenge in this regard is to social work which needs to reverse the profession's move away from a self-reflective reflective culture to promote personal as well as professional development for social work staff, including systematic critical reflection on the impact of their values, experiences and biographies on work with vulnerable fathers and families (Ferguson and Hogan, 2004, p. 183).

In cases that have not fully entered child protection systems and are on the cusp between welfare concerns and child protection, there is value in official acknowledgement of the benefits of using the voluntary sector. Page *et al.* note that:

> a small number of family services were working closely with the voluntary and community sector organisations. This was seen to help with: engaging some fathers who have negative perceptions of public services; providing alternative locations for provision; and tapping into networks of parents that voluntary and community sector organisations had already developed (Page *et al.*, 2008, p. 91).

Local authorities can make an explicit commitment to resource small support groups, specifically of the kind that provide services to fathers in need (many of whom will be involved with child welfare and protection). However, such a commitment rarely stretches to more long-term funding, which would secure provision. Often these small groups find local government monitoring and evaluation systems burdensome.

In relation to child protection concerns, research in the US concludes that:

> Agencies and courts should make clear what steps caseworkers should consider when mothers do not know or share information about the child's father. Even when mothers do provide information on the child's father, workers may want to reach out to other individuals (e.g. relatives, former caseworkers) in order to confirm and expand upon the information provided (Malm *et al.*, 2006, p. 164).

Such a policy challenges one of the more negative functions of the mother as gatekeeper – something that requires skilled handling but has proved to be successful in achieving the greater involvement of birth fathers in adoption (Loftus, 2004). Additional pointers include:

- Children's services ought to monitor the attendance of fathers (resident and non-resident) at child protection conferences and at meetings that plan and make decisions about children.
- Local authority education services should review whether the way services are structured actually creates obstacles to fathers (particularly non-resident fathers) being involved in their children's lives: for example, whether schools are required to communicate concerns about children's welfare

(e.g. inviting them to discuss a child's absences from school) to non-resident fathers.

- Research consistently shows that FGCs are more successful in involving fathers, father-figures and paternal relatives than statutory decision-making mechanisms. They are also more successful in producing plans for children that enable them to live safely within their family network, such as with a grandparent, when they cannot remain living with their mother or father. All authorities should provide a FGC service to address child welfare concerns, and all families should be offered a FGC prior to the local authority taking care proceedings.

Getting it right at team and agency levels will not be easy and, as indicated, this will take: a combination of culture shift about fathers (which is happening at a societal level); messages that central and local government policymakers 'get it'. The inclusion of a fathers' dimension in the Scottish national parenting strategy is a positive step; better-informed professionals; and perhaps one or two determined individuals. The rewards for children, women, fathers and families are potentially great.

Teaching programmes: Developing father-sensitive practice in social work education

> Education and training of child and family professionals needs to address head on dominant images of masculinity which regard men as non-nurturing beings – and all the more so if they carry markers of being the 'hard-man' on their bodies and demeanours – and which equate caring solely with femininity/motherhood (Ferguson and Hogan, 2004, pp. 9–10).

How and where should the subject of fathers be integrated in the education of social workers? Should there be separate or integrated lectures, that is, a stand-alone series of fathers' lectures or a permeated approach? As already noted, there are parallels between challenging father-exclusionary practices and early discussions about how to combat racism and discrimination. The latter were resolved with a strategy that sought to do both, and there is no reason why a similar approach cannot be adopted in social work training curricula. Students will benefit from specific input on fathers, but they will also gain from ensuring that, for example, when theories of attachment are discussed, children are not depicted as solely the responsibility of mothers. A US study of fathers in social work concludes that:

> Social work educators must review their reading materials to ensure that gender-biased literature is either not included or is addressed in class discussions. Textbooks that present theories of human behavior should include challenges to heavily relied-on traditional theories. Given that much of the research literature in child welfare has been (and still is) biased, course materials in such areas as sexual abuse and child welfare may need to be even more heavily scrutinised (Risley-Curtiss and Heffernan, 2003, p. 12).

A later Canadian study comes to similar conclusions:

> We surveyed thirty-two undergraduate social work programmes in Canada and reviewed their syllabi in family practice, child welfare, indigenous practice and human development courses to determine the content on fathers and fathering (Walmsley *et al.*, 2006). We found that fewer than 5% of courses related to children and family work mentioned fathers in any way (Brown *et al.*, 2009, p. 28).

The survey of the social work curriculum in the UK by Featherstone *et al.* (2010) identifies that fathers were not a priority within the curriculum: for example, fathers did not figure in the legal component of the courses; and gender was rarely emphasised. Human development, assessment and interventions were the most common areas on the curriculum where inputs on fathers were to be found. Less than a quarter of the programmes had any input on fathers on courses dealing with ethics or anti-oppressive practice. Under half of the programmes that responded to the survey (twelve) indicated that they did not teach about fathers in their law teaching. Of those who did include fathers in their law modules, two indicated it was brief or cursory and one that it was solely about domestic violence (Featherstone *et al.*, 2010, p. 54).

In a more recent piece in *Community Care*, one newly qualified social worker, who graduated from Brunel University in 2009, argues that: 'It's crucial that fathers' details are recorded and fathers are engaged with the services they and their families are accessing.' She continues that this did not come across in her degree:

> There's a lot of research on the importance of engaging with fathers but in my course there was never a module or a set period to talk about that … I don't want to minimise the effects of domestic violence, but the emphasis was around fathers as a danger to the family (quoted in Carson, 2011).

What exactly could father-inclusive education look like? Daniel and Taylor argue that: 'Before practitioners engage meaningfully with service users and clients they must have the opportunity to reflect upon their own values about children, parenting and gender' (Daniel and Taylor, 2001, p. 212) and that they ought to explore the question 'Do I have deep-seated suspicions about men?' (ibid.). It follows that the same opportunities for self-reflection should be made available for students to:

> critically reflect on their assumptions and attitudes towards men, women and gender roles, and their own experiences of being fathered, so that learning can occur about how these influence their understanding of masculinity and practice (Ferguson, 2011, p. 163).

Here are a few suggestions that would help develop father-inclusive practice on training programmes. The first is aimed at achieving the kind of reflection suggested by Daniel and Taylor (2001) and Ferguson and Hogan, (2004), by scheduling tutorials and seminars that consist of one-line questions, such as 'How do you remember your father?' and 'What was the most significant moment you remember with your father/male role model?' The ensuing discussion will undoubtedly be animated, and tutors/facilitators will have to ensure that any students should be advised of the topic in advance, and that there should be no compulsion to make personal contributions.

In addition to revising human growth and development materials, such as attachment and teaching the benefit of positive father involvement, lecturers and tutors should consider reviewing reading lists to include some of the material on fathers already referred to in this book; citations of otherwise important social work texts (e.g. Fahlberg's (2008) *A Child's Journey Through Placement*) should come with a proviso that they overlook fathers. The same approach should be applied to online teaching materials, such as that on assessment developed by the Scotland-based Institute for Research and Innovation in Social Services (2007), which, in a scenario of a young girl's life from being 'looked after' and accommodated to her adoption and eventual entry to further education, manages to depict a life (Clapton, 2009). Other ways to ensure the inclusion of fathers are:

- The legislative framework materials could be revised to incorporate basic knowledge of father's rights, especially those fathers whose names are not on their child's birth certificate and non-resident fathers, and other fathers such as those who have overnight contact with their children (in other more orthodox circumstances it is normal for children to have friends for sleepovers, but can children on supervision who stay with their father for the weekend also have friends to sleep over?). Social work students also need a grounding in care proceedings and contact in fostering and adoption cases and, in Scotland, a knowledge of fathers' entitlements in the Children's Hearings system.
- Skills development work could include the kind of specifics that work best with men, which have been referred to in earlier chapters, such as humour and directness. Such activities ought also to tackle the 'fear factor' – the feelings and emotions that can be present when working with men who display aggressive or intimidating behaviours.
- When learning and teaching tools are devised or selected (e.g. vignettes, problem-based learning scenarios and case materials), lecturers could ensure that these do not solely portray fathers as absent, useless or a threat. See the previous discussions on how training materials can reflect or perpetuate one-dimensional notions of fathers.
- Service users' input could include contributions from fathers recruited from and supported by local fathers groups.

- The survey by Featherstone *et al.* (2010) called for placement opportunities for working specifically with fathers. If not wholly able to meet the demands of a placement, it may be that a student placement could incorporate one or two days a week work with a local fathers' group or project. Observational visits, inductions etc. should also include time with fathers' workers. In Aberdeen, social work students spend time with Dads Work, which specialises in helping fathers involved in the criminal justice system and those who substance misuse. See http://makinggenderequalityreal.org.uk/dads-work-%E2%80%93-neighbourhood-service-aberdeen-city (accessed 17 December 2012).
- Essay feedback to students ought to challenge descriptions that include phrases such as 'father is out of the picture'.

Food for thought in training and education

The role and influence of fathers has to date been overwhelmingly concentrated on fathers and their underage children. Is there a case for discussing fathers and fathering across the lifespan? There are many practice instances when relationships between fathers and their mature children come to the fore. In after-adoption work, for example, practitioners regularly mediate between older fathers and their adult children. In more mainstream statutory services, vulnerable men in the community may also be fathers, yet this part of their identity can be overlooked when assessments of needs and support are undertaken. Equally, parents of adults with learning disabilities may find that practice tends to focus on the mother, and as a result the father's contribution and responsibilities can be neglected.

We can also speculate about fathers who are in the criminal justice system. As noted previously, not only might they have a part to play in their children's welfare, but it may also be that work with these men and their identities as fathers, *irrespective of the age* of their children, may be fruitful. Across the gamut of social work practice other examples come to mind: for example, practice with adults who suffer a mental illness might also benefit from an exploration of how people cope with father or filial loss or absence. Such a joining up of practice thinking would need to be matched by a similar leap by policymakers, who continue to think in terms of the existing service delivery silos of children/offenders/adults, and here academics and researchers have a further role to play in reshaping policy thinking.

The next and final chapter of *Social Work with Fathers: Positive Practice* is about fathers' support organisations and for fathers' workers. The resources they provide are crucial at a very practical level for fathers and their families, and increasingly their voices are being heard at policy level.

Key research and resources

A Review of How Fathers Can be Better Recognised and Supported Through DCSF Policy, J. Page, G. Whitting, G. and C. Mclean (2008), especially Chapters 4 and 5. Available at URL: www.education.gov.uk/publications/eOrderingDownload/DCSF-RR040.pdf (accessed 17 December 2012)

For further recommendations for positive father practice at an agency level see the three valuable publications produced by the Family Rights Group:

Working with Risky Fathers: Fathers Matter 3: Research Findings on Working with Domestically Abusive Fathers and Their Involvement with Children's Social Care Services, C. Ashley (ed.) 2011);

Fathers Matter 2: Further Findings on Fathers and Their Involvement with Social Care Services, C. Roskill, B. Featherstone, C. Ashley and S. Haresnape (2008); and *Fathers Matter: Research Findings on Fathers and Their Involvement with Social Care Services*, C. Ashley, B. Featherstone, C. Roskill, M. Ryan and S. White (2006).

Fathers Matter: Resources for Social Work Educators, B. Featherstone, C. Fraser, B. Lindley and C. Ashley (2010, published by the Family Rights Group. Available at URL: www.swap.ac.uk/docs/fathersmatter.pdf (accessed 17 December 2012)

CHAPTER 7

For Fathers' Workers

There are many organisations and websites that offer advice and support to fathers and those working with them. The websites for these organisations provide links to many other local and regional groups that are either father-friendly or directly engaged in offering support to fathers and their families.

Fathers' organisations

The main UK-wide ones are the Fatherhood Institute and Families Need Fathers (FNF).

Fatherhood Institute

This offers a sophisticated range of help for fathers and professionals: for example, research summaries relating to child welfare and protection; and it engages in lobbying in the interests of fathers. The Fatherhood Institute's aims are:

- To change work so that fathers can be more available to care for their children. They want to see more fathers, including fathers on low incomes, working flexibly and part-time, and taking more leave off for caring.
- To change education so that boys are prepared for future caring roles, and boys and girls are prepared for the future sharing of these roles. The Fatherhood Institute wants to see children and young people discussing gender inequalities and understanding that mothers and fathers experience pressure to specialise in caring and earning roles, and that mothers and fathers should have a similar range of choices over their caring roles, not limited by gender. They want to see more encouragement of boys into childcare careers.

- To change supports to family life so that the caring role of fathers and father-figures is recognised and strongly supported. The Fatherhood Institute wants laws, policies and public services to encourage and enable fathers to invest more of their time and energy in the direct care of their children. They want all health, education, family and children's services to be 'father-inclusive' – that is, to support fathers in their caring roles as seriously as they currently support mothers. See www.fatherhoodinstitute.org (accessed 17 December 2012).

Families Need Fathers

A second UK-wide, high-profile organisation is FNF, which focuses most of its work on fathers' rights, especially in relation to divorce, separation and custody issues. FNF has a number of UK branches, which offer the *pro bono* advice of solicitors and others familiar with the family courts. It describes itself as:

> chiefly concerned with the problems of maintaining a child's relationship with both parents during and after family breakdown. We offer information, advice and support services for parents who could otherwise spend thousands of pounds without achieving a positive outcome for the children (see www.fnf.org.uk; accessed 17 December 2012).

Fathers Network Scotland

In 2010, a national Scottish organisation was established entitled Fathers Network Scotland (FNS). FNS describes itself as a collection of professionals, dads and individuals interested in fatherhood who have come together to help support men in their role as fathers in Scotland. The objectives of FNS are to:

- promote the physical, mental and emotional health of fathers in Scotland through the provision of support to men in all aspects of their role as fathers and to raise awareness and increase understanding of the importance of fathers in child development;
- advance education through the development and promotion of good practice in all aspects of work with fathers and the

production and dissemination of information and research related to fatherhood and work with fathers (see www.fathersnetwork.org.uk; accessed 17 December 2012).

Doing fathers' work

While researching and writing this book, I became aware that some of the material that I had gathered best belonged in a separate chapter for the individuals who are engaged in setting up a father's project, maintaining one or developing one. This chapter now discusses the role of these fathers' workers, collates what we know works best and shares some suggestions for development.

Sometimes poorly funded, sometimes funded for very short terms, there are many such people throughout the UK. They can be men or women and have a number of titles: for example, dads' worker, fathers' development co-ordinator, fathers support worker. The work is invaluable and yet, as noted by Lewis and Lamb (2007), much of it goes either unrecorded or is not evaluated and then publicised. Networks such as FNS have an important role to play in offering a clearing house for information exchange, so workers can communicate with each other. In an interesting development, FNS has set up a peer support service for fathers' workers in recognition of the fact that, in their day-to-day support and advice-giving capacity, they are often faced with emotionally demanding and taxing cases, some of which may involve serious child welfare and protection matters. The opportunity to share concerns is proving highly valued by the workers who use the service.

Aside from the networks and national organisations, what about the aims and needs of the individual fathers' worker? Successful fathers work needs clarity as to the primary focus. But is it necessarily with fathers? What about successful fathers' work with mothers? Children? The family? What might be another non-father focus? Changes in thinking within the team or agency? Practice changes among the professionals and agencies within the local area? Broader influence on policymakers?

Whether some or all of the above are part of the job of a fathers' worker, much of the time they will be engaged in developing or facilitating groups.

Doing fathers' work – in groups

Typically the group work-related activities of a fathers' worker will include: recruitment, planning sessions, out-of-group activities, evaluation and, when there is the time, sharing good practice. More often than not, the above activities will occur alongside considerable effort in raising funds for the maintenance and development of the initiative. In addition, according to circumstances, a fathers' worker may also find that a great deal of their time and energy can be spent in lobbying and persuading others in the agency or within their local council of the importance of engaging with fathers.

For every type of father and every type of fathering challenge, there has been or is a group or service. There are those that offer support and advice for fathers-to-be through to grandfathers. There are groups for lone fathers, black and minority ethnic fathers, young fathers and stepfathers. Research indicates that successful fathers' activities (whether concerning the project as a whole or the group work undertaken) include the following factors:

- a clearly defined conceptual framework (what is the purpose of the group?, how would success be measured by a potential participant?);
- respected leadership;
- preparedness for intensive intervention with the most vulnerable fathers;
- 'savvyness' regarding lobbying;
- a number of targets and strategies for action to achieve these;
- a governance framework (is there a 'secretary' needed, who will be the treasurer?);
- quality partnerships with agencies and individuals in these bodies;
- stable and diversified funding (adapted from Bolté *et al.*, 2001).

Project workers have to respect the fact that there are biological differences between men and women, and there are also variations in the way they socialise. As a result, different strategies are necessary to reach men and get them to make a commitment to a group. Men's competitive nature needs to be taken into account, and there should be a focus more on action: for example, sitting around in a circle and talking just does not work with young fathers – the event has to be fun. Young fathers will participate all the better if the activity or session comes with some humour.

Activities need to be structured in such a way that young fathers always feel comfortable enough to be able to say what they're feeling. Some styles of interaction and communication seem to work best. Any fathers' group facilitator, for example, will have to ensure they are accessible, approachable and aware of the fact that they are not a specialist who has an answer to everything. A female facilitator will have to take care not to arouse feelings of distrust among fathers' wives or girlfriends, and all facilitators have to make fathers' participation easier: for example, occasionally fathers should be treated like guests, and their transportation costs or entrance fees for outings taken care of. One fathers' worker explains his successes thus:

> I think my whole approach is a bit more loose with fathers. I want them to be aware that the program has objectives to attain, but, at the same time, the atmosphere has to be a bit more informal and relaxed than with mothers. It's quite funny, I have more fathers that usually knock on my door – just show up on their lunch hour to ask something about fathering – while mothers usually call first before coming. Men are also a bit more reserved, more stand-offish. They will go and have a look at the bulletin board but they won't stop at an information booth if there is someone there to discuss the hand-outs with them. And fathers define participation more flexibly: for them the word doesn't necessarily mean that they come to every single activity but that they participate in the program more or less regularly throughout the year, or even participate in other activities set up by other services from the same agency (quoted in Bolté *et al.*, 2001, p. 115).

This worker goes on to say that the fathers who participate:

> know they have a place in the project, that they are welcome and won't be rejected. Here, a man can bang his fist on the table without people automatically thinking he's a violent person (Bolté *et al.*, 2001).

RUNNING A FATHERS' GROUP WHEN YOU ARE A WOMAN

'Working with a male clientele helped VandenBroek better understand what it's like to be a minority, such as when men visit organizations in which the staff is mostly women. However, she has a warning for female staff: "Try to work through your own personal biases first before sitting around the table with men. If you have personal biases men are going to pick up on that right away." On the other hand, the men tell her that as a facilitator and a mother, she helps them see things more objectively. They say that the fact that they are not involved emotionally or physically with her helps them to better understand the father's role from a mother's standpoint. VandenBroek feels that there is one other positive aspect of men and women working together: "Having a male/female facilitation team is positive in any group; it allows you to provide positive models of communication between men and women."

Paradoxically, having a woman facilitator is less of a problem for the fathers than it is for people outside the project. VandenBroek says that her presence is often wrongly interpreted, and that society creates barriers to men and women working together because they scrutinize their behaviour much more than they do in single-gender environments' (Bolté *et al.*, 2001, p. 99).

If facilitated carefully, there is much therapeutic content in groups that on the surface may appear to be 'just guys and their kids getting together'. In Edinburgh, Dads Rock meets every Saturday morning for an hour and half and ends with fathers and children goofing around to 'We will rock you' by Queen. In between, there is crawling on hands and knees, cups of tea and standing about. Just under the surface, men are exchanging tips about nappy rash, sleep patterns and managing sleepovers when you do not have primary custody.

Fathers' groups can cover a spectrum of collective activities: some of them will be social, usually meeting with their children and involving activities such as Dads Rock and trips out; others will be behaviour-based, where violent and/or abusive behaviour may be the focus. Further ones will be more explicitly therapeutic, where open discussion, use of personal experiences and exploration of masculinity and personal development are characteristic. Other groups will be educational, concentrating on child development, parenting skills and issues (how to discipline effectively) and life skills (communication, decision-making, dealing with stress, relationship issues, health and sexuality); these groups may also have an advocacy/advice function and might involve guest speakers or staff and participants sharing their own expertise. Yet more groups may be more goal-directed, where men engage in activities designed to produce a particular outcome or product (e.g. planning a family event; producing a booklet/DVD about local services or about their experiences; and designing a new playground for their children). Fathers' projects might offer all of the above in overlapping activities: for example, what is ostensibly an opportunity for fathers to look after a gardening plot (with and without their children) can become a setting wherein much healing may take place between men and between fathers and children. Fathers' workers will pay attention to the importance of low-cost activities such as this and, for example, just walking. Dads Work in East Lothian organises no-cost guided walks.

Children in Scotland have brought together a collection of practical tips on how projects have successfully engaged with fathers (see 'Practical tips for establishing and running a fathers' group'). Much of these have already been discussed in previous chapters on reaching and working with fathers; however, tips include attention to the importance of workers offering one-to-one opportunities for fathers. There will be much demand on fathers' workers to provide such help, because group work alone will not meet the diversity of needs of fathers who may either get in touch or be referred.

PRACTICAL TIPS FOR ESTABLISHING AND RUNNING A FATHERS' GROUP

- Getting timing and place right – daytime, evening and weekend sessions suit fathers in different circumstances; crèche facilities may be required, depending on the activity; location needs to be accessible; and negative associations (e.g. with formal education or agencies) may put some dads off attending.
- Being proactive – e.g. carrying out home visits; arranging transport to venues or meeting points; having an identified and accessible contact person who is prepared to build relationships; and following up with fathers after an initial contact or a course has ended.
- Using 'hooks' to engage fathers in the first instance – competitions through schools, gala days, cooking, sports and outdoor activities have all been used. Fathers Day and National Play Day are good opportunities

to engage with fathers and children. The weekly Forest Nursery in Fife has proved very popular with dads and has led to an increased uptake of parenting workshops by dads.

- Participation is voluntary, not compulsory – involvement should be portrayed as a normal 'parenting' activity, not as a punishment for being a 'bad' father.
- Building trust – differentiating support or activities offered from formal education (with which some participants will have had poor experiences) and agencies; making it clear that the group's and/or workers' approach is (and remains) non-judgemental; and ensuring confidentiality is maintained within a group (especially important where sensitive issues are being discussed).
- Valuing dads' own experiences, learning and pooled knowledge over that of 'experts' – parenting support should be about engaging with dads, not lecturing.
- Offering one-to-one support and advocacy across a range of areas (e.g. housing, benefits, debt, health, finding work, education/training opportunities) – can also include signposting to other specialist sources of advice and support.
- Allowing fathers' (and/or children's) needs and wishes to lead – in terms of pace, activities, subjects for discussion and format. In parenting support, models and programmes can provide useful elements/building blocks, but they tend to work best when treated as adaptable, not as inflexible blueprints.
- Facilitating the important social function of groups – the fathers' group is not all about learning or interaction with a specific service; promoting peer support, a sense of belonging and fun are also important.
- Organising a range of engaging, low-cost activities for fathers and children (e.g. visits to local attractions, camping trips, photography projects, cooking, meals together, badminton, competitions, circus skills, aromatherapy, health checks).
- Embracing challenging issues and topics (e.g. abuse, addiction, separation) – in providing parenting support, it is important to give fathers the opportunity to explore personal issues, including their own experiences as children, so they are able to understand better and consider their current role as fathers and to work out where and how to do things differently.
- Building broader skills (i.e. non-parenting) development into a programme of support – e.g. group facilitation skills, education and training (Allen and Jones, 2010).

Doing fathers' work – with individuals

For all the reasons discussed in previous chapters – child protection, parenting challenges and advocacy – fathers' workers can be overrun with referrals and can become a dumping ground for every man who local agencies do not know how to work with. It is, therefore, important to pay careful attention to what can be taken on and what cannot. Some of this will be trial and error, and fathers' workers may find themselves combining the roles of counsellor, lawyer and social worker.

Fathers' projects often deal with basics previously done by social workers, such as organise the provision of beds and bedding, and they provide food and toys when faced with impoverished fathers who want to provide for their children who are coming for an overnight stay. However, it is the individual work with fathers that may occupy a great deal of the time. Men whose children have been taken into care who feel loss and shame, fathers who have struck their children and partners, fathers who are angry about 'the system' and so on, all benefit best from someone who can listen, contain their anger and grief and also challenge them. Day in and day out, in the course of offering a therapeutic and confidential space for men to talk, fathers' workers (if they are doing their job) may experience dilemmas such as whether or not to alert others to information shared about violence in the home, benefit fraud or what they might believe to be mental ill health in need of intervention. They will bear witness to, already indicated, anger but also frustration and despair. For all these reasons peer support, coaching, clinical supervision – whatever term may be used – is essential for fathers' workers.

Finally, another service that may be provided by fathers' workers is that of accompanying professionals on visits: for example, to health visitors. Sometimes, this may arise out of a perception of threat of violence or perhaps because the man is known or recorded as (not the same thing) an 'angry father'. Whatever the particular request or challenge, fathers' workers need to have a clear notion of what they are prepared to do and how thin they can be spread.

Doing fathers' work – without fathers

A 'dedicated' service for fathers may include work on helping an existing service to become more father-friendly. Where to start, for example, if given the task of improving young fathers' experiences of maternity services? This could mean drawing up and distributing fliers and hoping that these young men will turn up at a meeting. However, a more productive approach might not focus on men so much as changing practice *within* maternity services. Many young fathers already attend scans and even antenatal classes, the welcome that young fathers receive at these points of contact could make all the difference as to whether they returned and became further committed to the process and the welfare of their partner and unborn children. An example of the kind of work achieved with the involvement of fathers' workers is the collaboration between Scottish fathers' projects and the National Childbirth Trust (NCT), in which a fathers' worker and NCT facilitator jointly run antenatal classes. A booklet has also been produced (see Davidson *et al.*, 2011).

In addition to other agencies and professionals, important work facilitating father–child relationships is often with other family members. Some of the most invaluable work supporting father–child relationships is done by people who work with mothers. As previously discussed, mothers can often have a significant influence on how much time the father and child spend together, whether they value each other, and how they use their time together. Therefore, while respectful of mothers' feelings and experiences, fathers' workers may find themselves exploring with mothers what the father can contribute to family life, and how he can be enabled to do that – and questioning low expectations and hostility towards him (or men in general). Alternatively, it may mean helping a mother in a new relationship think about children's relationships with stepfathers and biological fathers.

In addition to fathers, professionals and other service users, fathers' workers can receive a great deal of attention from the media, especially around Fathers Day or the launch of an initiative around a hot topic, such as storytelling for fathers and children. Less frequently but depending on the political climate, fathers' workers and projects may find their views being sought by local and national government or may wish to make their views known. The Fatherhood Institute regularly lobbies governments, and one successful campaign activity bore fruit in 2012, when the UK government agreed to trial joint birth registration. Currently, while a mother is always recorded on the birth certificate, the father is only recorded if the mother consents – either by marrying him or, if they are not married, by consenting to his signing the birth certificate (see www.fatherhoodinstitute.org/2012/joint-birth-registration-is-on-its-way-a-big-victory-for-children-dads-and-the-fi; accessed 17 December 2012). Elsewhere, also in 2012, FNS was invited by the Scottish government to take part in discussions to shape a national parenting strategy.

All these demands mean that fathers' workers can be hugely overworked: once their existence is known, everyone may want a piece of them. It also suggest that fathers and fathering, and the benefits of positive involvement of fathers, are on the agenda to an extent that has not been seen in the past. This helps offset the evenings when only two fathers turn up at the group, and workers have to remind themselves that simply keeping going may actually be a measure of success.

SOME LAST WORDS

All contemporary writing on fathers begins by acknowledging the enormous growth in interest in this area. This book has sought to balance messages for policymakers with suggestions for practitioners. It has also tried to walk a line between a 'how to' manual and review of up-to-date research findings. It has endeavoured to be readable for those who work with fathers and those who write about them. It is hoped that both food for thought and action will be the result.

What fathers do, how they do it, and how we think about and understand fathering has changed. While not yet having the hands-on caring connotations of mothering, fathering as a caring and nurturing activity is now an accepted role for men at home, outside the school gates, in parks and playgrounds and in the streets and shopping centres. Notions of the distant, emotionally constrained or strict disciplinarian father, and of men who do not know one end of a baby from another, are constructs of the twentieth century and not of this one. Not all fathers do well. Some will struggle; some may resist; and some may be too occupied with earning or with careers to be the best fathers they could be. However, not all mothers manage this, either. Women do not and should not bear sole responsibility for the nurture of children.

Our ideas about fathers need to be refreshed to reflect changing times and mores. Stereotypical views of men as absent or uncaring need to be sensitively revisited not least in policy and practice and related guidance in the child protection and childcare sector. This does not mean denying some of the problem areas in families and relationships. What it does entail is that it is important to recognise stereotypes and assumptions about fathers, and about mothers, have no place in work with families, and that they reinforce deficits rather than promote positive change. This is especially true in children and family services. Policymakers and practitioners should work on the basis that fathers can and do make an essential contribution to family life and can be, and are, as central to the well-being of children as mothers.

REFERENCES

Action for Prisoners' Families (2010) Facts and Figures about Prisoners' Families, London: Action for Prisoners' Families

Allen, K. and Jones, K. (2010) *Breaking-down Stereotypes and Engaging Fathers in Services for Children and Families*, Children in Scotland. Available from URL: http://makinggenderequalityreal.org.uk/wp-content/uploads/gedreportv9_ged.pdf (accessed 17 December 2012)

Amato, P. and Sobolewski, J. (2004) 'The effects of divorce on fathers and children: Non-residential fathers and stepfathers', in Lamb, M. (ed.) (2004) *The Role of the Father in Child Development*, New Jersey: Wiley

Ashley, C., Featherstone, B., Roskill, C., Ryan, M. and White, S. (2006) *Fathers Matter: Research Findings on Fathers and Their Involvement with Social Care Services*, London: Family Rights Group

Ashley, C. (ed.) (2011) *Working with Risky Fathers: Fathers Matter 3: Research Findings on Working with Domestically Abusive Fathers and Their Involvement with Children' Social Care Services*, London: Family Rights Group

Asmussen, K. and Weizel, K. (2010) *Evaluating the Evidence: Fathers, Families and Children*, London: National Academy for Parenting Research, King's College

Australian Fatherhood Research Network (2009) *Father-inclusive Practice Guide*, Canberra: Australian Government Department of Families, Housing, Community Services and Indigenous Affairs

Bakermans-Kranenburg, M., van Ijzendoorn, M. and Juffer, F. (2003) 'Less is more: Meta-analyses of sensitivity and attachment interventions in early childhood', *Psychological Bulletin*, Vol. 129, No. 2, pp. 195–215

Barker, G. (2006) 'Men's participation as fathers in Latin America and the Caribbean: Critical review of the literature and policy options', in Bannon, I. and Correia, M. (eds) (2006) *The Other Half of Gender: Men's Issues in Development*, Washington, DC: The International Bank for Reconstruction and Development/The World Bank

Bartlett, D. and Vann, N. (2004) 'Review of the state of practical work', in *Supporting Fathers: Contributions from the International Fatherhood Summit 2003*, The Hague, The Netherlands: Bernard van Leer Foundation

Bayley, J., Wallace, L. and Choudhry, K. (2009) 'Fathers and parenting programmes: Barriers and best practice', *Community Practitioner*, Vol. 82, No. 4, pp. 28–31

Baynes, P. and Holland, S. (2012) 'Social work with violent men: A child protection file study in an English local authority', *Child Abuse Review*, Vol. 21, No. 1, pp. 53–65

Bellamy, J. (2009) 'A national study of male involvement among families in contact with the child welfare system', *Child Maltreatment*, Vol. 14, No. 3, pp. 255–62

Berlyn, C., Wise, S. and Soriano, G. (2008) *Engaging Fathers in Child and Family Services. Participation, Perceptions and Good Practice*, Canberra, Australia: National Evaluation Consortium, Social Policy Research Centre, at the University of New South Wales, and the Australian Institute of Family Studies

Blanden, J. (2006) *'Bucking the Trend': What Enables Those Who are Disadvantaged in Childhood to Succeed Later in Life?*, Norwich: Department for Work and Pensions

Bolté, C., Devult, A., St-Denis, M. and Gaudet, J. (2001) *On Fathers' Ground: A Portrait of Projects to Support and Promote Fathering*. Available at URL: www.phac-aspc.gc.ca/hp-ps/dca-dea/publications/father-pere/pdf/father_e.pdf (accessed 17 December 2012)

Bowman, D., Scogin, F. and Floyd, M. (2001) 'Psychotherapy length of stay and outcome: A meta-analysis of the effect of therapist sex', *Psychotherapy*, Vol. 38, No. 2, pp. 142–8

Bradshaw, J., Skinner, C., Stimson, C. and Williams, J. (1999) *Absent Fathers?*, London: Routledge

Braithwaite, J. (2002) *Restorative Justice and Responsive Regulation*, New York: Oxford University Press

Brandon, M., Bailey, S., Belderson, P., Gardner, R., Sidebotham, P., Dodsworth, J., Warren, C. and Black, J. (2009) *Understanding Serious Case Reviews and Their Impact: A Biennial Analysis of Serious Case Reviews 2005–07*, Norwich: University of East Anglia

Bronte-Tinkew, J., Burkhauser, M. and Metz, A. (2008) *Elements of Promising Practice in Teen Fatherhood Programs*, Washington, DC: US Department of Health & Human Services

Brown, L., Callahan, M., Strega, S., Walmsley, C. and Dominelli, L. (2009) 'Manufacturing ghost fathers: The paradox of father presence and absence in child welfare', *Child & Family Social Work*, Vol. 14, No. 1, pp. 25–34

Buchanan, A. (1996) *Cycles of Child Maltreatment: Facts, Fallacies, and Interventions*, Chichester: John Wiley

Bunting, L. (2005) *Teenage Parenting: Professional and Personal Perspectives*, Dissertation, Belfast: School of Social Work, Queen's University

Burgess, A. (2005) 'Fathers and public services', in Stanley, K. (ed.) (2005) *Daddy Dearest: Active Fatherhood and Public Policy*, London: Institute for Public Policy Research

Burgess, A. (2010) *Young Fathers*, presentation Fatherhood Institute. Available at URL: www.emotionaldevelopment.co.uk/store/files/AdrienneBurgessYOUNGFATHERBrighton2010.ppt (accessed 17 December 2012)

Burnside, J. (2006) *A Lie About My Father*, London: Cape

Cameron, D. (2011) 'PM David Cameron says "runaway dads" should be "shamed" ', *The Sunday Telegraph*, 18 June 2011. Available at URL: www.bbc.co.uk/news/uk-13825737 (accessed 4 January 2013)

Campbell, A. (2012), 'We need society to value fathers, says children's minister', *The Scotsman*, 18 June 2012. Available at URL: www.scotsman.com/the-scotsman/scotland/we-need-society-to-value-fathers-says-children-s-minister-1-2360894 (accessed 4 January 2013)

Carson, G. (2011) 'Tackling social workers' anti-men attitudes', *Community Care*, 15 April. Available from URL: http://www.communitycare.co.uk/articles/15/04/2011/116687/tackling-social-workers-anti-men-attitudes.htm (accessed 4 January 2013)

Chang, L., Schwartz, D., Dodge, K. and McBride-Chang, C. (2003) 'Harsh parenting in relation to child emotion regulation and aggression', *Journal of Family Psychology*, Vol. 17, No. 4, pp. 598–606

Children's Workforce Development Council (2010) *The Team Around the Child (TAC) and the Lead Professional: Trainer Notes*, Leeds: Children's Workforce Development Council

Christie, A., (2001) *Men and Social Work: Theories and Practice*, Hampshire: Palgrave

Clapton, G. (2003a) *Birth Fathers and Their Adoption Experiences*, London: Jessica Kingsley

Clapton, G. (2003b) *How Do You Remember Your Father? How Will Your Children Remember You?: The Healthy Fathering Project 2000–2002*, Stirling: Aberlour

Clapton, G. (2009) 'How and why social work fails fathers: Redressing an imbalance, social work's role and responsibility', *Practice: Social Work in Action*, Vol. 21, No. 1, pp. 17–34

Clapton, G. (2012) 'Scottish fathers: An absence in Scottish policies', in Simpson, C. (ed.) (2012) *Scotland: The Best Place in the World to Bring Up Children?*, Edinburgh: Parenting Across Scotland

Connell, R. (1995) *Masculinities,* California: University of California Press

Connor, M., White, J. and Caldwell, L. (eds) (2006) *Black Fathers: An Invisible Presence in America*, Mahwah, NJ: Lawrence Erlbaum

Cornwall, A. (2000) 'Missing men? Reflections on men, masculinities and gender in GAD', *IDS Bulletin*, Vol. 31, No. 2, pp. 18–27

Cullen, S., Cullen, A., Band, M., Davis, L. and Lindsay, G. (2010) 'Supporting fathers to engage with their children's learning and education: An under-developed aspect of the parent support adviser pilot', *British Educational Research Journal*, Vol. 37, No. 3, pp. 485–500

CWDC (2010) *The Team Around 98the Child (TAC) and the Lead Professional: Trainer Notes*, Salford: Children's Workforce Development Council

Daniel, B. and Taylor, J. (2001) *Engaging with Fathers: Practice Issues for Health and Social Care*, London: Jessica Kingsley

Davidson, M., Cooper, K., Brough. A. and Allen, K. (2011) *Dads2b: A Resource for Professionals Providing Antenatal Education and Support to Fathers,* Children in Scotland, NHS Lothian, National Childbirth Trust and West Lothian Sure Start. Available at URL: www.childreninscotland.org.uk/docs/13302Dads2bResource_A-2.pdf accessed 17 December 2012)

De Boer, C. and Cody, N. (2007) 'Good helping relationships in child welfare',

Child and Family Social Work, Vol. 12, No. 1, pp. 32–42

Dennis, N. and Erdos, G. (1992) *Families Without Fatherhood*, IEA Health and Welfare Unit. Available at URL: www.civitas.org.uk/pdf/cs03.pdf (accessed 17 December 2012)

Department of Economic and Social Affairs of the United Nations Secretariat (2011) *Men in Families and Family Policy in a Changing World*, New York: United Nations

Dermott, E. (2008) *Intimate Fatherhood: A Sociological Analysis*, London: Routledge

Dominelli, L., Strega, S., Walmsley, C., Callahan, M. and Brown, L. (2011) ' "Here's my story": Fathers of "looked after" children recount their experiences in the Canadian child welfare system', *British Journal of Social Work*, Vol. 41, No. 2, pp. 351–67

Donnelly, P., Williams, D., Boyle, P., Leyland, A. and Nicholls, E. (2010) *Youth Male Violence in Scotland: Understanding Antecedents, Reducing Recidivism, and Tackling Health Inequalities*, St Andrews: University of St Andrews

Dunn J., Cheng, H., O'Connor, T. and Bridges L. (2004) 'Children's perspectives on their relationships with their non-resident fathers: Influences, outcomes and implications', *Journal of Child Psychology and Psychiatry and Allied Disciplines*, Vol. 45, No. 3, pp. 553–66

Edwards, T. (2006) *Cultures of Masculinity*, London: Routledge

Ellison, G., Barker. A. and Kulasuriya T. (2009) *Work and Care: A Study of Modern Parents*, Manchester: EHRC

English, D., Brummel, S. and Martens, P. (2009) 'Fatherhood in the child welfare system: Evaluation of a pilot project to improve father involvement', *Journal of Public Child Welfare*, Vol. 3, No. 3, pp. 213–34

Fabiano, G. (2007) 'Father participation in behavioral parent training for ADHD: Review and recommendations for increasing inclusion and engagement', *Journal of Family Psychology*, Vol. 21, No. 4, pp. 683–93

Fahlberg, V. (2008) *A Child's Journey Through Placement*, London: British Association for Adoption and Fostering

Family Commission (2009) *Supporting Kiwi Dads*, Family Commission Report 5/09, New Zealand: Family Commission

Farmer, E. and Owen, M. (1998) 'Gender and the child protection process', *British Journal of Social Work*, Vol. 28, No. 4, pp. 545–64

Farrant, F. (2006) *Out for Good: Resettlement Needs of Young Men in Prison*, London: Howard League for Penal Reform

Fatherhood Institute (2009a) *Commissioning Father-Inclusive Parenting Programmes: A Guide*, Abergavenny: Fatherhood Institute

Fatherhood Institute (2009b) *Fathers and Parenting Interventions: What Works?* Abergavenny: Fatherhood Institute

Fatherhood Institute (2010a) *Fatherhood Institute Research Summary: Fathers' Impact on Their Children's Learning and Achievement*, Abergavenny: Fatherhood Institute

Fatherhood Institute (2010b) *Fatherhood Institute Research Summary: Young Fathers*, Abergavenny: Fatherhood Institute

Fathers Direct (2004a) *Inside Fatherhood*, London: Fathers Direct

Fathers Direct (2004b) *Working with Fathers: A Guide for Practitioners in Family and Community Services*, London: Fathers Direct

Fathers Direct (2007) *Ten Top Tips for Father-inclusive Practice*. Available at URL: www.fatherhoodinstitute.org/2007/ten-top-tips-for-father-inclusive-practice (accessed 17 December 2012)

Fathers Direct (2008) *The Costs and Benefits of Active Fatherhood*, London: Fathers Direct

Featherstone, B. (2003) 'Taking fathers seriously', *British Journal of Social Work*, Vol. 33, No. 2, pp. 239–54

Featherstone, B. (2004) *Family Life and Family Support: A Feminist Analysis*, Basingstoke: Palgrave Macmillan

Featherstone, B. (2009) *Contemporary Fathering: Theory, Policy and Practice*, Bristol: Policy Press

Featherstone, B. (2010) 'Engaging fathers – promoting gender equality?', in Featherstone, B., Hooper, C-A., Scourfield, J. and Taylor, J. (eds) (2010) *Gender and Child Welfare in Society*, Chichester: Wiley-Blackwell

Featherstone, B., Fraser, C., Lindley, B. and Ashley, C. (2010) *Fathers Matter: Resources for Social Work Educators*, London: Family Rights Group

Featherstone, B., Rivett, M. and Scourfield, J. (2007) *Working with Men in Health and Social Care*, London: Sage

Feder, L. and Wilson, D. (2005) 'A meta-analytic view of court mandated batterer intervention programs: Can courts affect abuser's behaviour?', *Journal of Experimental Criminology*, Vol. 1, pp. 239–62

Ferguson, H. (2011) *Child Protection Practice*, Basingstoke: Palgrave Macmillan

Ferguson, H. and Hogan, F. (2004) *Strengthening Families Through Fathers: Developing Policy and Practice in Relation to Vulnerable Fathers and Their Families*, Waterford, Republic of Ireland: The Centre for Social and Family Research, Waterford Institute of Technology

Finkelhor, D., Moore, D., Hamby, S. and Strauss, M. (1997) 'Sexually abused children in a national survey of parents: Methodological issues', *Child Abuse and Neglect*, Vol. 21, No. 1, pp. 1–9

Fisher, J., Cabral de Mello, M., Patel, V. and Rahman, A. (2006) 'Maternal depression and newborn health', *Newsletter for the Partnership of Maternal, Newborn & Child Health*, Issue 2, Geneva

Flouri, E. (2005) *Fathering and Child Outcomes*, Chichester: Wiley

Flouri, E. and Buchanan, A. (2002) 'Father involvement in childhood and trouble with the police in adolescence: Findings from the 1958 British cohort', *Journal of Interpersonal Violence*, Vol. 17, No. 6, pp. 689–701

Franck, E. (2001) 'Outreach to birthfathers of children in out-of-home care', *Child Welfare*, Vol. 80, No. 3, pp. 381–99

Funder, K. (1996) *Remaking Families: Adaptation of Parents and Children to Divorce*, Melbourne: Australian Institute of Family Studies

Garbers, C., Tunstill, J., Allnock, D. and Akhurst, S. (2006) 'Facilitating access to services for children and families: Lessons from Sure Start local programmes', *Child and Family Social Work*, Vol. 11, No. 4, pp. 287–96

Gillies, J. (2004) 'Fathers and hearings', in *Children's Panel National School: What Price Dads?*, Proceedings 29–31 October 2004 at Hilton Dunblane Hydro, Dunblane; Aberdeen: University of Aberdeen

Gilligan, P., Manby, M. and Pickburn, C. (2012) 'Fathers' involvement in children's services: Exploring local and national issues in "Moorlandstown"', *British Journal of Social Work*, Vol. 42, No. 3, pp. 500–18

Gingerbread (2012) 'Who's the daddy? Charity puts single fathers in the picture', Press release, 15 June

Giveans, D. and Robinson, M. (1992) 'Old and new images of fatherhood', in Scull, C. S. (ed.) (1992) *Fathers, Sons, and Daughters: Exploring Fatherhood, Renewing the Bond*, Los Angeles: Jeremy P. Tarcher

Glover, J. (2009) *Every Night You Cry: The Realities of Having a Father in Prison*, Ilford: Barnardo's

Goff, S. (2012) 'The participation of fathers in child protection conferences: A practitioner's perspective', *Child Abuse Review*, Vol. 21, pp. 275–84

Goldman, R. (2005) *Fathers' Involvement in their Children's Education*, London: National Family and Parenting Institute

Guille, L. (2004) 'Men who batter and their children: An integrated review', *Aggression and Violent Behavior*, Vol. 9, No. 2, pp. 129–63

Guterman, N. and Lee, Y. (2005) 'The role of fathers in risk for physical child abuse and neglect: Possible pathways and unanswered questions', *Child Maltreatment*, Vol. 10, No. 2, pp. 136–49

Hango, D. (2007) 'Parental investment in childhood and educational qualifications: Can greater parental involvement mediate the effects of socioeconomic disadvantage?', *Social Science Research*, Vol. 36, No. 4, pp. 1371–90

Harper, C. and McLanahan, S. (2004) 'Father absence and youth incarceration', *Journal of Research on Adolescence*, Vol. 14, No. 3, pp. 369–97

Harris, K., Furstenberg, F. and Marmer, J. (1998) 'Paternal involvement with adolescents in intact families: The influence of fathers over the life course', *Demography*, Vol. 35, No. 2, pp. 201–16

Hawkins, A. and Belsky, J. (1989) 'The role of father involvement in personality change in men across the transition to parenthood', *Family Relations*, Vol. 38, No. 4, pp. 378–84

Hawkins, A. and Dollahite, D. (1997) 'Beyond the role inadequacy perspective of fathering', in Hawkins, A. and Dollahite D. (eds) (1997) *Generative Fathering: Beyond Deficit Perspectives*, Thousand Oaks, CA: Sage

Haywood, C. and Mac an Ghail, M. (2003) *Men and Masculinities*, Buckingham: Open University Press

Her Majesty's Inspectors of Prisons (1997) *Thematic review of young prisoners by HM Chief Inspector of Prisons for England and Wales*, London: HMSO

Hirsch, D. (2006) *What Will It Take To End Child Poverty? Firing On All Cylinders*, York: Joseph Rowntree Foundation

Huebner, R., Werner, M., Hartwig, S., White, S. and Shewa, D. (2008) 'Engaging fathers', *Administration in Social Work*, Vol. 32, No. 2, pp. 87–103

Hughes, B. (2008), Minister of State for Children, Young People and Families,

8 January 2008. Available at URL: http://news.bbc.co.uk/1/hi/uk/7175673.stm (accessed 17 December 2012)

Institute for Research and Innovation in Social Services (2007) *The Assessment Triangle*. Available at URL: http://content.iriss.org.uk/assessment/triangle.html (accessed 17 December 2012)

Johnson, D. (1996) *Father Presence Matters: A Review of the Literature*, Philadelphia, PA: National Center on Fathers and Families

Kalil, A., Ziol-Guest, K. and Coley, R. (2005) 'Perception of father involvement patterns in teenage mother families: Predictors and links to mothers' psychological adjustment', *Family Relations*, Vol. 54, No. 2, pp. 197–211

Kandiyoti, D. (1988) 'Bargaining with patriarchy', *Gender and Society*, Vol. 2, No. 3, pp. 274–90

Katz, A. (ed.) (2002) *Parenting Under Pressure: Prison*, London: Young Voice

Kimmel, M., Hearn, J. and Connell, R. (eds) (2005) *Handbook of Studies on Men and Masculinities*, Thousand Oaks, CA: Sage

Kiselica, M. (2008) *When Boys Become Parents: Adolescent Fatherhood in America*, New Brunswick, NJ: Rutgers University Press

Krishnakumar, A. and Black, M. (2003) 'Family processes within three-generation households and adolescent mothers' satisfaction with father involvement', *Journal of Family Psychology*, Vol. 17, No. 4, pp. 488–98

Lamb, M., Pleck, J., Charnov, E. and Levine, J. (1987) 'A biosocial perspective on paternal behavior and involvement', in Lancaster, J., Altmann, J., Rossi, A. and Sherrod, L (eds) (1987) *Parenting Across the Lifespan*, New York, NY: Aldine de Gruyter

Lee, K. (2005) 'Fatherhood across the life course: Paternal careers and generational change', paper presented at the CRFR conference for new researchers in families and relationships, 25 October

Lee, S., Bellamy, J. and Guterman, N. (2009) 'Fathers, physical child abuse, and neglect', *Child Maltreatment*, Vol. 14, No. 3, pp. 227–31

Lewis, C. and Lamb, M. (2007) *Understanding Fatherhood: A Review of Recent Research*, York: Joseph Rowntree Foundation

Livia Sz, A., Bernhardt, E. and Goldscheider, F. (2002) 'Co-residential paternal roles in industrialized countries: Sweden, Hungary and the United States', in Hobson, B. (ed.) (2002) *Making Men into Fathers: Men, Masculinities and the Social Politics of Fatherhood*, Cambridge: Cambridge University Press

Lloyd, N., O'Brien, M. and Lewis, C. (2003) *Fathers in Sure Start*, London: Institute for the Study of Children, Families and Social Issues, University of London

Loftus, C. (2004) 'Changes in birth father involvement in stepfamily adoption in the Republic of Ireland', *Adoption and Fostering*, Vol. 28, No. 1, pp. 59–69

Loucks, N. (2012) 'Prison and parenting', in Simpson, C. (ed.) (2012) *Scotland: The Best Place in the World to Bring Up Children?*, Edinburgh: Parenting Across Scotland

Loughton, T. (2010), Parliamentary Under-Secretary of State for Children and Families, 11 November 2010. Available at URL: www.education.gov.uk/inthenews/speeches/a0067212/tim-loughton-to-the-fatherhood-institute

(accessed 17 December 2012)
Lundahl, B., Tollefson, D., Risser, H. and Lovejoy, M. (2008) 'A meta-analysis of father involvement in parent training', *Research on Social Work Practice*, Vol. 18, No. 2, pp. 97–106
Malm, K., Murray, J. and Green, R. (2006) *What About the Dads? Child Welfare Agencies' Efforts to Identify, Locate and Involve Non-resident Fathers*, Washington, DC: US Department of Health and Human Services, Office of the Assistant Secretary for Planning and Evaluation
Marsiglio, W. and Hinojosa, R. (2010) 'Stepfathers' lives: Exploring social context and interpersonal complexity', in Lamb, M. (ed.) (2010; 5th edn) *The Role of the Father in Child Development*, Hoboken, NJ: Wiley
Marsiglio, W. and Pleck, J. (2005) 'Fatherhood and masculinities', in Kimmel, M., Hearn, J. and Connell, R. (eds) (2005) *The Handbook of Studies on Men and Masculinities*, Thousand Oaks, CA: Sage
Maxwell, N., Scourfield, J., Featherstone, B., Holland, S. and Lee, J. (2012a) 'The benefits and challenges of training child protection social workers in father engagement', *Child Abuse Review*, Vol. 21, No. 4, pp. 299–310
Maxwell, N., Scourfield, J., Featherstone, B., Holland, S. and Tolman, R. (2012b) 'Engaging fathers in child welfare services: A narrative review of recent research evidence', *Child & Family Social Work*, Vol. 17, pp. 160–9
McKeowen, K., Ferguson, H. and Rooney, D. (1998) *Changing Fathers? Fatherhood and Family Life in Modern Ireland*, Cork: Collins Press
McLanahan, S. and Teitler, J. (1999) 'The consequences of father absence', in Lamb, M. (ed.) (1999) *Parenting and Child Development in 'Nontraditional Families'*, Mahwah, NJ: Lawrence Erlbaum
Meek, R. (2004) 'Parenting education for young fathers in prison', *Child & Family Social Work*, Vol. 12, No. 3, pp. 239–47
Meek, R. (2011) 'The possible selves of young fathers in prison', *Journal of Adolescence*, Vol. 34, No. 5, pp. 941–9
Miller, W. and Rollnick, S. (2002) *Motivational Interviewing*, New York: Guilford Press
Minnesota Fathers & Families Network (2007) *Do We Count Fathers in Minnesota?* Minnesota, MN: Child and Family Studies Department, St Cloud State University
Morgan, D. (1992), *Discovering Men*, London: Routledge
Morgan, D. (1998) 'Risk and family practices: Accounting for change and fluidity in family life', in Silva, E. and Smart, C. (eds) (1998) *The New Family?*, London: Sage
Morran, D. (2011) 'Re-education or recovery? Re-thinking some aspects of domestic violence perpetrator programmes', *Probation Journal*, Vol. 58, No. 1, pp. 23–36
National Child Welfare Resource Center for Family-Centered Practice (2002) *Best Practice Next Practice: Family-centred Child Welfare*, Washington, DC: Children's Bureau
Neil, E. (2000) 'The reasons why young children are placed for adoption: Findings from a recently placed sample and a discussion of implications for

subsequent identity development', *Child & Family Social Work*, Vol. 5, No. 4, pp. 303–16

O'Brien, M. (2005) *Shared Caring: Bringing Fathers into the Frame*, London: Equal Opportunities Commission

O'Donnell, J. M., Johnson, W. E., Jr., D'Aunno, L. E. and Thornton, H. L. (2005) 'Fathers in child welfare: Caseworkers' perspectives', *Child Welfare*, Vol. 84, pp. 387–414

O'Hagan, A. (1999) *Our Fathers*, London: Faber and Faber

Page, J., Whitting, G. and Mclean, C. (2008) *A Review of How Fathers Can Be Better Recognised and Supported Through DCSF Policy*, Research Report DCSF-RR040, London: Department for Children, Schools and Families

Palkovitz, R. (2002) *Involved Fathering and Men's Adult Development: Provisional Balances*, Mahwah, NJ: Lawrence Erlbaum

Parke, R., Dennis, J., Flyr, J., Morris, K., Killian, C. and McDowell, D. (2004) 'Fathering and children's peer relationships', in Lamb, M. (ed.) (2004; 4th edn) *The Role of the Father in Child Development*, Hoboken, NJ: John Wiley

Peacey, V. and Hunt, J. (2009) *I'm Not Saying It Was Easy … Contact Problems in Separated Families*, London: Gingerbread

Peled, E. (2000) 'Parenting by men who abuse women: Issues and dilemmas', *British Journal of Social Work*, Vol. 30, No. 1, pp. 25–36

Perel, G. and Peled, E. (2008) 'The fathering of violent men: Constriction and yearning', *Violence Against Women*, Vol. 14, No. 4, pp. 457–82

Pleck, J. (2007) 'Why could father involvement benefit children? Theoretical perspectives', *Applied Development Science*, Vol. 11, No. 4, pp. 196–202

Pleck, J. and Masciadrelli, B. (2004) 'Paternal involvement by U.S. residential fathers: Levels, sources and consequences', in Lamb, M. (ed.) (2004; 4th edn) *The Role of the Father in Child Development*, Hoboken, NJ: John Wiley

Plumtree, A. (2011) 'Children's hearings: Whether father "a relevant person"', *Adoption and Fostering*, Vol. 35, No. 1, pp. 81–2

Pritchard, C., Davey, J. and Williams, R. (2012) 'Who kills children? Re-examining the evidence', *British Journal of Social Work*. Advance access published 3 May 2012 available from URL: http://bjsw.oxfordjournals.org/content/early/2012/05/03/bjsw.bcs051.abstract (accessed 4 January 2013)

Quinlivan, J. and Condon, J. (2005) 'Anxiety and depression in fathers in teenage pregnancy', *Australian and New Zealand Journal of Psychiatry*, Vol. 39, No. 10, pp. 915–20

Radhakrishna, A., Bou-Saada, I., Hunter, W., Catellier, D., and Kotch, J. (2001) 'Are father surrogates a risk factor for child maltreatment?', *Child Maltreatment*, Vol. 6, No. 4, pp. 281–9

Real, T. (1997) *Don't Want To Talk About It: Overcoming the Secret Legacy of Male Depression*, New York, NY: Fireside Press

Reid, J. and Murphy, T. (2009) 'Lost identities and the need for a framework for intervention', paper to the international conference on Children and the law: International approaches to children and their vulnerabilities. Available at URL: http://eprints.hud.ac.uk/8505/1/ReidLostpdf.pdf (accessed 17 December 2012)

Risley-Curtiss, C. and Heffernan, K. (2003) 'Gender biases in child welfare', *AFFILIA*, Vol. 18, No. X, pp. 1–15

Rivett, M. (2010) 'Working with violent male carers (fathers and stepfathers)', in Featherstone, B., Hooper, C.-A., Scourfield, J. and Taylor, J. (eds) (2010) *Gender and Child Welfare in Society*, Chichester: Wiley-Blackwell

Rosenberg, J. and Wilcox, W. (2006) *The Importance of Fathers in the Healthy Development of Children*, Washington, DC: National Clearinghouse on Child Abuse and Neglect Information Children's Bureau/ACYF

Roskill, C. (2011) 'Research in three children's services authorities', in Ashley, C. (ed.) (2011) *Working with Risky Fathers: Fathers Matter; Vol. 3: Research Findings on Working with Domestically Abusive Fathers and Their Involvement with Children's Social Care Services,* London: Family Rights Group

Roskill, C., Featherstone, B., Ashley, C. and Haresnape, S. (2008) *Fathers Matter 2: Further Findings on Fathers and Their Involvement with Social Care Services*, London: Family Rights Group

Ross, E. (2006) *Engaging with Fathers – Men in the FGC Process*, Edinburgh: Children 1st

Rouch, G. (2005) *Boys Raising Babies: Adolescent Fatherhood in New Zealand*, Wellington: FAIR Centre of Barnardo's, New Zealand

Russell, G., Barclay, L., Edgecombe, G., Donovan, J., Habib, G. and Callaghan, H. (1999) *Fitting Fathers into Families: Men and the Fatherhood Role in Contemporary Australia*, Canberra, ACT: Department of Family and Community Services

Ruxton, S. (ed.) (2004) *Gender Equality and Men: Learning from Practice*, London: Oxfam

Ryan, M. (2000) *Working with Fathers*, Abingdon: Radcliffe Medical Press

Sanders, M. (2009) 'Fatherhood and recovery', *The Source*, Vol. 19, No. 1, pp. 14–16

Sarkadi, A., Kristiansson, R., Oberkliad, F. and Bremberg, S. (2008) 'Fathers' involvement and children's developmental outcomes: A systematic review of longitudinal studies', *Acta Paediatrica*, Vol. 97, pp. 153–8

Scott, K. and Crooks, C. (2004) 'Effecting change in maltreating fathers: Critical principles for intervention planning', *Clinical Psychology: Science and Practice*, Vol. 11, No. 1, pp. 95–111

Scottish Government (2009) *The Early Years Framework*, Edinburgh: Scottish Government

Scottish Government (2010) *National Guidance for Child Protection in Scotland*, Edinburgh: Scottish Government

Scottish Government (2012) *A Guide to Getting It Right For Every Child*, Edinburgh: Scottish Government

Scourfield, J. (2001) 'Constructing men in child protection work', *Men and Masculinities*, Vol. 4, No. 1, pp. 70–89

Scourfield, J. (2006) 'The challenge of engaging fathers in the child protection process', *Critical Social Policy*, Vol. 26, No. 2, pp. 440–9

Scourfield, J., Maxwell, N., Holland, S., Tolman, R., Sloan, L., Featherstone, B. and Bullock, A. (2011) *A Feasibility Study for a Randomised Controlled Trial of a Training Intervention to Improve the Engagement of Fathers in the Child Protection System*, Cardiff: National Institute for Social Care and Research

Sheldon, S. (2007) *A Socio-Legal Analysis of Fatherhood: Full Research Report*, ESRC end-of-award report RES-000–27–0111, Swindon: Economic and Social Research Council

Sherriff, N. (2007) *Supporting Young Fathers*, Brighton: The Trust for the Study of Adolescence

Silverstein, L. and Auerbach, C. (1999) 'Deconstructing the essential father', *American Psychologist*, Vol. 54, No. 6, pp. 397–407

Smith, M., Clapton, G. and Schinkel, M. (2011) *Skilling Up: Educating & Training for Residential Child Care*, Edinburgh: University of Edinburgh

Sonenstein, F., Malm, K. and Billing, A. (2002) *Study of Fathers' Involvement in Permanency, Planning and Child Welfare Casework*, Washington, DC: US Department of Health and Human Services

Stanley, N., Graham-Kevan, N. and Borthwick, R. (2012) 'Fathers and domestic violence: Building motivation for change through perpetrator programmes', *Child Abuse Review*, Vol. 21, pp. 264–74

Stover, C., Meadows, A. and Kaufman, J. (2009) 'Interventions for intimate partner violence', *Professional Psychology: Research and Practice*, Vol. 40, No. 3, pp. 223–33

Strega, S., Fleet, C., Brown, L., Dominelli, L., Callahan, M. and Walmsley, C. (2008) 'Connecting father absence and mother blame in child welfare policies and practice', *Children and Youth Services Review*, Vol. 30, No. 7, pp. 705–16

Strug, D. and Wilmore-Schaeffer, R. (2003) 'Fathers in the social work literature: Policy and practice implications', *Families in Society*, Vol. 84, No. 4, pp. 503–11

Sullivan, A. and Dex, S. (2009) *Millennium Cohort Study Sweep 3 Scotland Report*. Available at URL: www.scotland.gov.uk/socialresearch (accessed 17 December 2012)

Thoburn, J., Lewis, A. and Shemmings, D. (1995) *Paternalism or Partnership? Family Involvement in the Child Protection Process*, London: HMSO

Thoennes, N. (2003) 'Family group decision making in Colorado', *Protecting Children*, Vol. 18, Nos 1–2, pp. 74–80

Trinder, L. and Lamb, M. (2005) 'Measuring up? The relationship between correlates of children's adjustment and both family law and policy in England', *Louisiana Law Review*, Vol. 65, pp. 1509–37

Velazquez, S. and Vincent, S. (2009) 'Strengthening relationships between non-resident fathers and their children', *The Source: Fostering Father Involvement Issue*, Vol. 19, No. 1, pp. 8–10

Velleman, R. (2004) 'Alcohol and drug problems in parents: An overview of the impact on children and implications for practice', in Gopfert, M., Webster, J. and Seeman, M. (eds) (2004; 2nd edn) *Seriously Disturbed and Mentally Ill Parents and Their Children*, Cambridge: Cambridge University Press

Walmsley, C. (2009) *Fathers and the Child Welfare System*. Available at URL: www.mcgill.ca/files/gender-child-welfare/FathersandChildWelfareSystemMar09.pdf (accessed 17 December 2012)

Weinman, M., Buzi, R. and Smith, P. (2005) 'Addressing risk behaviours, service needs and mental health issues in programs for young fathers', *Families in Society*, Vol. 86, No. 2, pp. 261–6

Wilson, G., Gillies, J. and Mayes, G. (2004) *Fathers as Co-Parents: How Non-resident Fathers Construe Family Situations*, Glasgow: Department of Psychology, University of Glasgow

Young, K. and Nathanson, P. (2012) 'But are the kids really all right?: Egalitarian rhetoric, legal theory and fathers', *New Male Studies: An International Journal*, Vol. 1, No. 1, pp. 61–82

Zelenko, M., Huffman, L., Lock, J., Kennedy, Q. and Steiner, H. (2001) 'Poor adolescent expectant mothers: Can we assess their potential for child abuse?', *Journal of Adolescent Health*, Vol. 29, No. 4, pp. 271–9

INDEX

Note: page numbers in *italics* denote figures or tables

abandonment xiii, 68, 69
Aberdeen social work students 81
absent father xiii, 11, 21, 25–6, 56
abuse 12, 57, 65
  see also sexual abuse
adoption 15, 76–7, 80, 81
adoptive father 2
advocacy for fathers 53, 75, 90
aggression towards social workers 53, 55
alcoholism 56
Allen, K. 90
Asmussen, K. 11–12, 29, 54
assessment of risk 59–61, 62
attachment 6, 14, 37, 39, 78
attitudes to fathers 14, 17–20, 36–8, 39–40, 58–9, 74–5
  see also positive practice with fathers
Auerbach, C. 19–20
Australian Fatherhood Research Network 40
Australian study 45–6

Baby P. case 33
Barnardo's study 48
Bartlett, D. 37, 75
Bayley, J. 28
Baynes, P. 16
Bellamy, J. 14, 28, 74
biological father xi, 1, 5–6, 15
  see also birth fathers
birth certificates, named father xi, 53, 80, 93
birth fathers 15–16, 74, 76–7
  see also biological father
Black, M. 44
Blanden, J. 10, 11
Bolté, C. 86, 87, 88
Bowlby, J. 19–20
boyfriends 67
Bradshaw, J. 45
Brandon, M. 33, 57–8
breadwinner role 4, 19
Brown, L. 20
Brunel University 79
Buchanan, A. 11
bullying 11, 50–1
Bunting, L. 42
Burgess, A. 27
Burnside, J.: *A Lie About My Father* xiii

Cameron, D. xiii
Campbell, A. xii
Canada
  child protection practice 16, 18–19
  social work programmes 78
care proceedings 14, 77
care staff 31–2, 74–5, 83–4
Caring Dads 70–1
caring role 59, 77, 83, 84
Carson, G. 79
Child Abuse Potential Inventory 11
child protection xiv, 13–14
  attitudes to fathers 14, 18, 58–9
  boyfriends/surrogate fathers 67
  Canada 16, 18–19
  dangerous fathers 56–7
  father-inclusive practice 29, 73
  fathers' exclusion 16
  positive practice 67–8
  training materials 20–4

USA 76
child protection case conferences 57
child welfare workers 48–9
childcare x–xi, 31–2, 83–4
child-centred assessment 57, 63–4
child–father relations 17, 36, 49, 92
children in care 16, 80, 91
Children in Scotland 89
Children's Hearings 12, 24, 80
Children's Panels *24*
Children's Workforce Development Council (CWDC) 20
A Child's Journey Through Placement (Fahlberg) 80
Clapton, G. vi, 6, 20, 50, 80
How Do You Remember Your Father? 39
Cody, N. 40
Community Care 79
Connor, M. 5
consciousness-raising 74
conversation model of work 38
Cornwall, A. 7
criminal justice system 48, 81
Crooks, C. 63, 64
custody issues 2, 84
CWDC (Children's Workforce Development Council) 20

Dads Rock 88
Dads Work 81, 89
dangerous fathers xiii, 56–7, 62, 63–4
Daniel, B. 38, 64, 79
daughters–fathers 17
see also child–father relations
DCSF (Department for Children, Schools and Families) 19
De Boer, C. 40
deficit assumptions approach 37–8
Dennis, N. 10
Department for Children, Schools and Families (DCSF) 19
depression 13, 25, 68
Dermott, E. 1
divorce 84
Dollahite, D. 17, 37–8
domestic violence 16, 27, 42, 43, 56
Dominelli, L. 18–19
donor insemination 1
drug use 42–3
see also substance misuse
Duluth model 69

early childhood 10–11, 68
The Early Years Framework, Scottish Government 70
Edinburgh project, lone fathers 52
education
father-inclusive 84
local authorities 76–7
poverty 10, 11
social work 79–80
emotions, repressed 68–9
engagement with fathers 32–5, 37, 38–40, 43, 61–6
English, D. 28
English as a second language 53
Erdos, G. 10
Erikson, E. 20
exclusionary practices 16, 32, 44

Fahlberg, V.: *A Child's Journey Through Placement* 80
Families Need Fathers (FNF) 83, 84
Families Outside 48
Family Commission 17
Family Group Conferences (FGCs) 70, 71, 77
family images, father-free 22, *23*
Family Rights Group (FRG) 16, 26, 53
Fathers Matter: Resources for Social Work Educators 82
Fathers Matter 2 82
Working with Risky Fathers 82
family services 75–6
Farrant, E. 41
father support groups 76
father-facing services 48
father-figure 3, 14, 67
fatherhood vi–vii, xi. xii–xiv, 1–3

early 43
masculinity 6–8
selflessness 41–2
sentencing 51
service provision 9
Fatherhood Institute xii, 83–4
father-inclusive policies 72
group meetings 31–2
involvement benefits 12, 13
lobbying government 93
practitioners 48
website 53
young fathers 43
fathering
belief in 26–7
criminal justice system 48
masculinity 7–8
as role 94
women in workforce 5
father–mother relationship 29–31, 44
fathers xi–xii
awareness of negatives 75
on birth certificates xi, 53, 80, 93
child protection practitioners 14
and children 17, 36, 49, 92
Children's Hearings 12
depression 68
finding 27–9
grown-up children 81
maltreatment assessment 59–61
overlooked 56, 80
own childhood 38–9
as protectors 57
as risk 32, 53, 55–6
role of vi, x, 57, 81
stereotypes xiii–xiv, 94–5
unaware of birth 45
see also attitudes to fathers; involvement; positive practice
Fathers Day xii, xiii, 92
Fathers Direct 9, 71, 74
fathers' group facilitators 87
fathers' groups
activities 88, 90
participation 87, 90
practical tips 89–90
run by woman 88
service users' input 80
therapeutic/educational 88–9
fathers in prison 39, 48–51, 53
Fathers Matter: Resources for Social Work Educators (FRG) 82
Fathers Matter 2 (FRG) 82
Fathers Network Scotland (FNS) 84–5
fathers' organisations 83–5
father's rights 7, 80
fathers' workers 72–3, 85, 86–90, 91, 92–3
fear factor 80
Featherstone, B. 30, 36, 37, 47, 61, 78, 81
feminist analysis 19
Ferguson, H. 12–13, 16–17, 19, 27, 32, 38–9, 44, 46, 51–2, 62, 74, 75, 77, 79
FGC (Family Group Conferences) 70, 71, 77
Flouri, E. 11
FNF (Families Need Fathers) 83, 84
FNS (Fathers Network Scotland) 84–5
Forest Nursery 90
fostering 2, 15–16, 80
Franck, E. 68
FRG (Family Rights Group) 16, 26, 53
Funder, K. 45–6

Gascoigne, P. xii
gatekeeper role 36, 44
gay fathers 53
gender issues 6–7, 67, 78, 79, 83, 86
Getting It Right For Every Child (Scottish Government) 70
Gilligan, P. 31, 41, 73
Gingerbread 45, 52
Giveans, D. 3
grandparents 25, 44
Greenock prison 50
group meetings

Fatherhood Institute 31–2
fathers' workers 85, 86–90
young fathers 43, 87
Guterman, N. 43

Harper, C. 16
Hawkins, A. 17, 37–8
Heffernan, K. 78
HMP Parc, Learning Together Project 51
Hogan, F. 12–13, 16–17, 19, 32, 38–9, 44, 46, 51–2, 62, 74, 75, 77, 79
Holland, S. 16
homelessness 11, 41
homemaker role 19
household father 5
How Do You Remember Your Father? (Clapton) 39
Huebner, R. 68
Hughes, B. xi–xii

imprisonment risk 16
inclusion of fathers 29, 55, 72, 73, 84
income, reduced 11
Incredible Years 54
Institute for Research and Innovation in Social Services 80
invisible father syndrome 27–8
involvement 3–6
belief in 26–7
child protection 29
children's education 10
children's later lives 11–12
gains for father 12, 13
non-resident fathers 11–12, 28–9
policy-making 15
social work practice 9, 15–24
types 3–4
US project 27–8
Irish studies 62

Johnson, D. 46
Jones, K. 90

Kalil, A. 11
Kiselica, M. 40–1, 43
Krishnakumar, A. 44

Lamb, M. 3–4, 4–5, 11, 85
learning disabilities 53, 81
Learning Together Project 51
Lee, K. 4
Lee, S. 57
Lee, Y. 43
legal father 1, 5
Lewis, C. 4–5, 11, 85
A Lie About My Father (Burnside) xiii
Livia Sz, A. 5
Livingstone, K. xii
local authorities 14, 15, 26, 73, 76–7
lone father 2–3, 52
Loucks, N. 48, 51
Loughton, T. xii

Mc Lanahan, S. 16
male carers 59
male childcare workers 31–2, 83–4
Malm, K. 18, 28, 30, 61, 73, 76
maltreatment 56, 59–61, 63, 64–5, 67
Marriage and Parenting in Stepfamilies Intervention 54
masculinity xii–xiii, 6–8, 74, 77, 88
Maslow, A. 20
maternity services 92
Maxwell, N. 58, 74
Meek, R. 50
Mellow Dads 71
Minnesota Fathers and Families Network 1–3
minority ethnic fathers 53
Morgan, D. 4, 7
Morran, D. 69
mothers
biological 5–6
depression 13, 25
father–child relationships 12–13, 92
as gatekeeper 36, 44, 76
homemaker role 19
as lead parent 29–30

sole responsibility 21
stress 11, 13
young 11, 41, 42
motivational interviewing 58
Mullen, P.: *Neds* xiii
multiple fathers 66
Murphy, T. 67–8

National Child Welfare Resources Center for Family-Centered Practice 18
National Childbirth Trust (NCT) 92
National Guidance for Child Protection in Scotland, Scottish Government 70
NCT (National Childbirth Trust) 92
Neds (Mullen) xiii
neglect 12
Neil, E. 15
non-biological father xi, 52
non-resident father xiii, 2, 3, 44–8
anger at treatment 46
Australia 45–6
child protection 16
children in care 16
communicating with 28–9
fostering 16
interventions for 46–8
involvement 11–12, 28–9
maltreatment 60
and mothers 30
school communications 77
Social Services 47

O'Hagan, A. xiii
Ormiston Trust 50–1

Page, J. 12, 15, 16, 19, 26, 29, 72, 75–6
Palkowitz, R. 4, 7–8
parenting, harsh 10
parenting education 49–50
parents as term 74
paternal leave xi
patriarchal dividend 6–7
peer relationships 11, 85
Peled, E. 57, 62
Perel, G. 57
placement opportunities 81
play with fathers 10–11
Pleck, J. 12
policy-making 15, 20–4, 70, 81–2, 94–5
Polmont Young Offenders Institution 48
positive practice vi–vii, x, xiv, 6
attitudes to be changed 15, 26, 27, 34
child protection 67–8
components 58–62
dealing with violence 63–6
father-figures 33–4
fathers in prison 48–51
in the field 72–7
lone fathers 52
non-resident fathers 46–8
principles of 36–40
risky behaviour 32, 66
social worker training 73, 77–82
stepfathers 51–2
supervising of 67–70
young fathers 43
poverty 10, 11
presumed father 2
Pritchard, C. 52
putative father 1–2

Quarriers 22, *23*

rapport-building 40
reading difficulties 53
recidivism, reducing 13, 48–9
record-keeping, mother and father 74
Reid, J. 67–8
resident father 2
residential provision for children 14
responsibility xi, 3, 66
restorative justice 65
risk and resource assessment 16, 66
risky behaviour 32, 66
Risley-Curtiss, C. 78

Rivett, M. 33, 57, 59
Robinson, M. 3
Rogers, C. 20
Rosenberg, J. 18, 56, 58, 59
Roskill, C. 15–16, 32
Ross, E. 71
Russell, G. 17
Ryan, M. 16

Sanders, M. 68–9
schools 10, 16, 77
Scott, K. 63, 64
Scottish Government
  child protection guidelines 22, *23*
  The Early Years Framework 70
  Getting It Right For Every Child 70
  National Guidance for Child Protection in Scotland 70
Scourfield, J. 18, 30, 61
self-improvement 13
self-reflection 75
sentencing/fatherhood 51
serious case reviews analysis 33, 57–8
service users' input 80
sexual abuse 17, 56, 65
Sheldon, S. 1
Sherriff, N. 43
Silverstein, L. 19–20
single parents 2–3, 52
Smith, M. xiii
social fathers xi, 2, 5, 51–2
social work education 73, 77–82
social work practice
  aggression towards 53, 55
  attitudes to fathers 36–8, 77–81
  dangerous fathers 64–5
  involvement of fathers 9, 15–24
  male/female workers 19, 31–2
  non-resident fathers 47
  positive practice 73, 77–82
  risk and resource assessment 16
  self-reflection 75
  stepfathers 51–2
social work programmes, Canada 78
social work students, Aberdeen 81
socialisation 73, 86
son–father relationship 49
  see also child–father relations
Stanley, N. 64
stepfathers 2, 51–2
stereotypes xiii–xiv, 40–2, 75, 94–5
storytelling, from prison 50
Strega, S. 27, 55
strengths-based practice 37, 38–40, 69–70
substance misuse 56, 81
Supporting Families Initiative xi
Supporting Father Involvement Project 54
Sure Start Children's Centres 19
surrogate fathers 67

Taylor, J. 38, 64, 79
Think Family initiative 36–7
Triple P 54
two-parent approach 37

unemployment 10, 56
US child protection studies 18, 19, 76
US paternal involvement 27–8

Vann, N. 37, 75
Velazquez, S. 31
Vincent, S. 31
violence 53, 59, 61–6
  see also domestic violence
voluntary sector 75

Weizel, K. 11–12, 29, 54
welfare benefits 30
Welsh child protection studies 18
Wilcox, W. 18, 56, 58, 59
Wilson, G. 46
Working with Risky Fathers (FRG) 82

young fathers 11, 40–4
  advocacy 53
  group activities 43, 87

interventions 43–4
maternity services 92
positive practice 43
in prison 48
stereotypes 40–2
youth offending 12, 16

Zelenko, M. 11